The Many Sides of
HAPPY

Practicing the Art of Choosing Happy for Overcoming Adversity and Challenge to Live Your Best Life

Mieka J. Forte

The Many Sides of Happy
Copyright © 2019 by Mieka J. Forte

Mieka Forte Inc
PO BOX 51045 Milton Central PO
Milton ON
Canada
L9T 2P2

All rights reserved. The content of this publication, including but not limited to text, information, images, diagrams or commentary (collectively "Materials") are protected by copyright and other intellectually property laws under the Provincial law of Ontario, the Federal law of Canada and international law as applicable. No part of the Materials may be copied, modified, reproduced, stored in a retrieval system, or transmitted, in any form by any means, electronic, mechanical, photocopying, recording or otherwise, without the prior written consent of Mieka Forte."

"This publication is for informational purposes only. The publisher nor the author are engaged in rendering medical, financial, psychological, legal or other professional advice. This publication is not a substitute for professional advice. If professional assistance is required, the services of a competent professional should be sought. The publication does not establish a therapist-client relationship between you and the publisher or author and is not intended as a solicitation of such. Under no circumstances shall the publisher or author be liable to you or any other person for any indirect, special, incidental or consequential damages arising from your use of this publication."

tellwell

Tellwell Talent
www.tellwell.ca

ISBN
978-0-22880-794-0 (Paperback)
978-0-22880-795-7 (eBook)

DEDICATION

I want to express an abundance of gratitude to all those who supported and encouraged me along the way. There are not enough words in the English language to truly express how grateful I am to everyone who participated in my workshops, did yoga together, had coffee, tea or wine with me, went for walks, talked with me in the school playground after drop-off, or listened to me unpack and dream about one day publishing this book. I also am grateful to those who I love dearly that are no longer with me and yet played such a powerful role in teaching me about love, life, resilience and the foundations upon which this book is written.

There are three people, though, who played such an incredibly pivotal role; and to them, I dedicate this book...

My husband Ed, and my sons Tyler and Mason.

I love you all more than I ever thought possible. Because of your unwavering love, encouragement and support, writing this book became possible. Thank you.

Hey fellow readers,

Thank you so much for picking up this book. Beyond these pages, I would love the opportunity to connect with you over on social media. You will find me on:
instagram @ miekaforte
facebook @ miekaforteinc

For more information on my workshops and speaking engagements you can check out my website at:
www.miekaforte.com

Table of Contents

Dedication 3
INTRO: Why Choose Happiness? 7
Chapter 1: Choosing Happy Even When Times Are Tough 11
Chapter 2: Recognizing Your Choice in the Matter 15

PART ONE: HAPPINESS GROUNDWORK 23

Chapter 3: Affirmations and Attention 27
Chapter 4: Let's Get Physical 38
Chapter 5: MMMMMM FOOOOD! 47
Chapter 6: Meditation 54
Chapter 7: Random Acts of Kindness 63
Chapter 8: Journaling and Gratitude 67

PART TWO: HIGHER INTO HAPPINESS 73

Chapter 9: Defining Happy 76
Chapter 10: Roadblocks and the Other Side of Happy 84
Chapter 11: Clearing Out the Roadblocks 93
Chapter 12: Mind-Body-Spirit 102
Chapter 13: Many Sides of Me 122

PART THREE: LIVING HAPPY 135

Chapter 14: F**k It! 137
Chapter 15: Discipline and Consistency 138
Chapter 16: Forgiveness 140
Chapter 17: Calling Out the Excuses 143
Chapter 18: Life Makes No Promises 147
Chapter 19: Recognizing Privilege 150
Chapter 20: Asking for Help and Finding Connection 152
Chapter 21: Celebrations 154

Appendix A: The Happy Meditation Practice (10 mins) 159
Appendix B: The Happy Workout (20 mins) 161
Appendix C: The Happy Yoga Practice (20 mins) 169
Appendix D: Root Chakra Yoga Practice 184
Appendix E: Sacral Chakra Yoga Practice 190
Appendix F: Solar Plexus Yoga Practice 194
Appendix G: Heart Chakra Practice 203
Appendix H: Throat Chakra Practice 209
Appendix I: Brow Chakra Meditation 212
Appendix J: Crown Chakra Meditation 214
References 217

INTRO

Why Choose Happiness?

When did happiness become complicated? It's amazing how many conversations I've had where people have said, "I just want to be happy" or "I just want this person to be happy." Then there's the number of raised hands I get when I ask, "Who would like more happiness in their lives?" every time I teach a workshop or speak at an event. Guaranteed, at least 90% of the room want to be happier.

I remember distinctly when happiness lost its natural ability to show up in my own daily life. This shift wasn't instantaneous. As I reflect back, I see a slow progressive chipping away at my happiness until one day life seemed too much to bear. The shift from happiness being regularly present in my life to a long-lost far-off memory happened over time, through a compounding of experiences; some traumatic, some mundane.

Being uncaring and guarded towards life became my norm. I existed in a space of settling for whatever was presented to me; some of it harsh and heart-breaking, some of it not so bad. Either way, I was uninterested, desensitized, numb to it and numb to life. I settled into the perspective that 'life is shit and then you die'.

You may be wondering what this has to do with choosing happiness. The answer is *everything*. I became aware of happiness having many sides and our ability to choose to be happy during a dark and challenging time in my life. Awarded yet another experience to remind me that happiness eluded me, I experienced grief, anger and defeat so palpable that it could have manifested into an entire human being. Happiness, for me, or so I thought, had left the building, not because it was no longer available, but because I had let it. I had *let it*. Not on purpose, of course.

Yet I had bought into the story that happiness came in a specific package, then convinced myself I didn't have the access code.

I allowed myself to view life through the narrowest of lenses. Becoming aware of this new information was a punch to the gut, then a smack to the head. Despite my circumstances, I had a choice to bring happiness back in my life, I realized. Yes, grief, anger and fear had moved into my heart, but as I learned, that didn't mean happiness had to move out and move out permanently. In the same space as the thick, sticky, heavy emotions of sadness, anxiety and defeat, happiness could co-exist. Bizarre as it was, I concluded that perhaps there are *many sides* to happiness. This new understanding meant happiness could still form a part of the overall picture.

I would have to choose it, though. I would have to make space for it. I would have to fight for it. Not because someone told me I had to be happy, but because I truly wanted it. I didn't want happiness because I was *supposed* to want it or because finding happiness was the right thing to do. Even with what I was navigating at the time, being happy was genuinely important to me. And I would have to willingly embrace the idea that happiness existed within me somewhere alongside the other emotions.

All these discoveries led me to learn how I could uncomplicate happiness. And my path of choosing happiness was ignited. Over the next decade, I solidified my understanding of the possibilities of choosing to be happy through my work teaching Choosing Happy workshops, speaking on the subject and coaching people one-on-one. My own experiences with happiness exploded into sharing this work with thousands of people. The cool part is: the more I worked within the field of happiness, the more I was reminded that choosing happy really is up to us. I witnessed this in everyone I was privileged to work with and found myself wanting even more people to become aware that choosing happy was within their grasp, regardless of their past, their financial status or their career aspirations. And there we have the inspiration to write this book.

In *The Many Sides of Happy*, you will find research and insights into the science behind happiness. Being educated in the wisdom and knowledge of how to cultivate happiness is personal power, but to foster the *ability* to choose happy, it's imperative to understand that we are not just science experiments, our choices and outcomes are not dictated only by research or mathematical formulae. We are human beings with an incredible power called the human spirit. By tapping into the true essence of our humanness and what the human experience really means, along with the application of happiness science, we create a masterplan for a life where we choose happy.

Everyone has a different personal definition of what happiness is. It's important to know yours, if happiness is up there on your list of priorities. My definition is this: *the beautiful sensation of fulfillment, motivation, peace, power of being alive, and presence.*

The central philosophy of *The Many Sides of Happy* is to embrace and honor the spectrum of all the human emotions within us in order to move into happiness. Meaning: to feel our truest sense of happiness, we need to allow ourselves to be sad, angry, frustrated, disappointed, ambivalent, calm, peaceful... When we can acknowledge all the aspects of ourselves that make us who we are, we take a massive first step in gaining the power to influence our happiness and exercise our power of choice.

CHAPTER 1

Choosing Happy Even When Times Are Tough

For obvious reasons, I get a lot of questions around what I mean by 'choosing happy'. Am I implying that someone can 'undo' depression, anxiety or any other kind of mental health issue? To make it clear from the outset, no, absolutely not.

When I use the term 'choosing happy' throughout this book, it's about seeing where we hold the power to make choices in line with who we are and how we want our lives to be. Many of us don't realize it, but we all hold this personal power. Indeed, I discovered it when I was experiencing the excruciating pain of *powerlessness*.

I was in my third year of university and my dad had just retired from a life-long career at Ontario Hydro. Three weeks after his retirement commenced, he embarked on his dream road trip, retracing his steps to Uranium City in western Canada where he had come from 30 years prior. (Not my ideal retirement vacation, but it was his!) My dad had been away about a week when we received that 3am phone call no one wants to receive. It was from my uncle in Saskatoon. We were informed that my father had suffered a massive heart attack. He had gone 17 minutes without oxygen to his brain and was in a critical condition. By 8am that morning, my sister, stepmother and I were at the airport beginning a journey that would ultimately change my perspective on happiness forever...

On arrival at the hospital, we met briefly with the doctors who warned us that our father would look completely different to when we had last seen him; his left ventricle had suffered severe damage and a massive amount of his ventricular heart tissue was dead; he was in a coma and the extent of his brain damage was unknown. They weren't even sure if he would wake from his coma. Indeed, when we saw him, my dad was unrecognizable. His body was so incredibly swollen that his knuckles were no longer visible. He remained in this state for days.

As time passed, the medical staff let us know that the likelihood of him waking up from his coma was becoming increasingly slim. Then 10 days after his heart attack, they said he was breathing on his own, but no other mental or physical activity had improved. My father had signed a DNR form (meaning 'do not resuscitate'), and because he could breathe on his own, technically even a tube was considered using 'extreme measures' to keep him alive. To honour his wishes, therefore, the tube would have to be removed. The doctors' main concern was the risk of his throat closing when the tube was removed, potentially causing death. Nevertheless, they removed the tube from my dad's airway, and he continued to breathe on his own. It was a success.

More days passed where no further progress was made. Unless my father showed some kind of improvement, the lack of development was evidence enough for the doctors that his brain damage was too extensive and the likelihood of him waking up minimal. This meant his feeding tube would be removed too as per DNR requirements and my dad would be put on morphine for the next month or so, until he eventually starved to death. To say we were shattered would be an understatement.

Miraculously, within a day or so, we saw some progress. My dad's eyes opened slightly and fluttered. His fingers moved. Within a few more days, he developed the ability to sit up, smile and cry. With these changes, he was upgraded to 'awake and alert' status, but still not fully out of his coma. In this state, watching was horrific and heartbreaking. One moment, he would laugh hysterically at who-knows-what; the next moment, he would burst into tears. He had no ability to communicate verbally. It was just extreme emotions.

The doctors explained that his behavior was caused by damage to the frontal lobe from the lack of oxygen. It meant he didn't have control over his limbic system at the back of his brain where primal emotions are located. The doctors couldn't confirm if he was truly feeling pain, physical or emotional. Processing this was hard. We were unsure how much my dad may or may not be suffering.

Amazingly, quick shifts happened. The medical staff got him standing up. And after three long weeks, he was air-lifted back to Ontario. My dad spent another three months in the hospital recovering. He worked on re-learning how to feed himself, walk without support, read and so many other skills that we take for granted. We each took shifts to go and visit him each and every day. However, he was extremely confused and he went through phases of phoning me, my sister or my stepmother at least five times a day when we were at work and no one was at the hospital with him.

Finally, the day came when my father was released home. It felt like all our prayers had been answered and the nightmare was finally over. Unfortunately, we were not fully aware of the complexity of this particular nightmare. Although, my dad had regained some extensive abilities, he had not recovered his short-term memory or certain years of his long-term memory. After a few weeks at home relearning where everything was in the house, my dad began a challenging new habit...

By now, I had started back to university and would wake up early every day to commute into school. Each morning around 6am, I would hear my dad shuffling down the hall and knocking on my bedroom door. He would open it and stand there, confused and fear-stricken, then asked, "Who is that woman in my room? Where is your mother?"

To backtrack briefly, my mother had passed away when I was seven years old, nearly 14 years prior. And 'that woman' in his room was his wife, my stepmother. To hear him utter these words disturbed me. And every day I would sit down with him at the kitchen table to explain that my mom had passed away and he was now remarried. My dad would sit in complete shock each day, as though it was the first time he was being told the love of his life had died. He would be filled with questions like, "How did she die? Did she suffer? Where was her cancer?" I can't begin to imagine how often he asked my stepmother those same questions over and over.

While the first day this happened was the most unnerving, as it continued on for weeks, it became all-consuming. To say I was drowning in my emotions and stress would be putting it mildly. "University days are the best days of your life," people would say, as I watched friends having fun and felt so jealous as these days turned out to be some of my worst.

Then one day something clicked, something that has changed the entire trajectory of my life.

I was so fed up feeling sad and grief-stricken I decided I was simply going to find a way to be happy. I know this sounds overly simplistic, but I was so pissed and frustrated with life that I was done. I didn't feel happy immediately that's for sure, but my goal became bringing back happiness into my life, and I made some changes immediately.

Next morning, when I woke to the sound of my dad shuffling down the hall, I said to myself with the loudest voice I could: *"I am happy."* I repeated it over and over and over, through gritted teeth, clenched fists and deep, deep breaths. We had our usual conversation about my mother's passing, then I got in my car, cranked my music and danced my heart out.

After doing this for a few days, things began to shift. Nothing changed with regards to my dad, my university responsibilities or my job expectations, which were paying for my schooling. The external world stayed exactly the same. The change was inside of me. Just by doing these two simple actions, I felt lighter. As that sense of lightness grew gradually, I became more open to other actions that allowed me to feel good. Eventually, among the darkness, grief and challenge, I felt a glimmer of happiness.

That happiness was there all along, just waiting to be noticed. I could connect with it, not just with the anger and grief that I had become so used to feeling. It wasn't by luck or by good financial fortune (that's for sure) that I changed. It didn't depend on my dad getting better. Unfortunately, his story was never to play out that way. Eventually, he moved to a retirement home, then 10 years later, he died of liver cancer. To this day, it makes me sad to think of what happened to my dad. Yet, it doesn't get to stop me from also choosing happy.

The lesson of finding and connecting with my happy in one of the darkest times in my life has become my sense of purpose, a drive to live and thrive beyond my wildest expectations. At the end of those dark times, I was still alive. I could still be happy even if my heart had been broken, even I had experienced intense grief. I understood that my happiness was not in the hands of someone else. Instead, I held the key to unlock my greatest desire. I held the key. And so do you!

CHAPTER 2

Recognizing Your Choice in the Matter

To keep on moving forward on the path of choosing happy requires more work than simply saying "I am happy" and car dancing. Although I still do both of those and highly recommend them, because they are exceptionally powerful, another extremely important element is to be able to recognize the multitude of choices that we make every single day and how the smallest choice can be a massive catalyst in our own happiness. When we stay present, connected, reminded and aware of our gift to choose, we understand our ability to choose happy. This is a practice in mindfulness.

    Each time we step out of the present moment and worry about the future or ruminate on the past, we miss out on the potential of the choice we have right now. There will always be reasons you're thinking about the future or the past, but if choosing happy is important to you, you will need to practice being mindful in your daily life.

    One prevailing distractor that can easily pull us away from the power of choice is fear. When we struggle with a fear or a phobia, it is paralyzing. In the mor when that fear takes over and is in control, we eliminate any possibility of My son suffered from a severe phobia; when he saw what he was afr would shut down and be completely exhausted from the energy it t him to 'choose' to be unafraid in that moment would have been ir had to do an incredible amount of work to see where he cou¹ power, overcome his fear and eventually choose to move forward. Witnessing his courage through this process was painful but inspiring.

Fear itself is not a bad thing. Fear exists as a survival mechanism. If a carnivorous predator happened to be chasing you, the fear drives inside telling you to run would have been *crucial*. However, when we apply that feeling to non-life-threatening situations, such as sabotaging happiness through fear of the unknown, then fear is not a matter of survival. It's a means to missing out on an extremely beautiful and powerful part of life. I call this *other fear*.

'Other fear' is a beast. It can mess you up! I distinguish between the two, because when we separate survival fear from 'other fear', we create an opportunity to act, instead of feeling prisoner to the fear or convinced that it is in charge. Examples of 'other fear' include: being afraid of success, worrying what someone else might think if we pursue something we want, avoiding something new simply because it's unfamiliar, or the fear of failure. 'Other fear' doesn't imply that whatever is causing the fear isn't scary or hard; just that the likelihood of death or harm is low. Therefore, 'other fear' is something we can overcome or work with, instead of something we need to run from or avoid.

The idea of being able to choose our actions and in turn influence a happy life for ourselves is incredibly exciting. However, whenever there are several options, there is a possibility of making a mistake and that excitement can quickly turn to intense fear AKA 'other fear'. At times, the 'what if' becomes so overwhelming that any opportunity for choice is lost.

For many, the fear of making a mistake or experiencing loss is very real, because they have lived it before. Difficult circumstances have a potent negative impact, especially on our happiness, for obvious reasons. When we feel these deep hurtful feelings, it is so intense and convincing that happiness seems to come and go by chance, not by choice. It isn't surprising that many believe happiness appears in our lives by good fortune considering the root of the word: *hap* meaning 'luck'.

We all know that tragedies happen. However, in times of misfortune, is it possible to choose any kind of joy? You can probably guess by the title of this book that indeed we can. Many components come into play when making our choices, including having a solid understanding of where we draw true sustainable happiness from. I'll give you a hint: we can't buy it.

I can't pretend to understand others' reasons for not making happiness a part of lives. I can only relate from my own life experiences, which invoked an exceptional amount of fear, disappointment and defeat. Yet, I was still able to discover that choosing happy is truly possible, even from the depths of that darkness.

I didn't hear of positive psychology until many years after I had that major epiphany on my ability to choose my own happiness even in trying times. Some people genuinely do not want to be happy; and others want to be happy yet aren't aware of their ability to impact their own experience. There is a difference between people who own and understand that they don't want happiness and people who do not realize they can choose to be happy. I am going to assume you have picked up this book because you want to make choices to move you in the direction of your happiness. And you're not in the camp of consciously deciding to be unhappy.

When the awareness of 'other fear' surfaces, we understand logically that our fears are unwarranted, yet emotionally simply letting go of those fearful 'what if' feelings isn't always that easy. One way to overcome other fear related to happiness is to gather information on the benefits of happiness. In other words, to educate yourself on happiness. Understanding the impact that being happy can have on your health and the wellbeing of others helps to dissipate the circulating fears.

Through many years of running workshops and coaching around happiness, I've seen that guilt commonly surfaces as an emotion when people work toward their own happiness. Brené Brown, the academic and author who created awareness of vulnerability, discusses how guilt keeps us stuck and isn't a helpful emotion. Feeling guilty for seeking happiness isn't going to change the fact that others are unhappy. Guilt doesn't change *anything* at all. It just makes you feel like crap. There is hope for you if guilt is a familiar part of your happiness avoidance, though. As you delve into truly understanding, feeling and seeing the impact of being happy over the course of this book, the guilt factor begins to melt away. It doesn't mean you won't feel empathy for those who are struggling, but it does mean you will no longer punish yourself for feeling good.

In his book *Flourish*, Martin Seligman provides insight on the positive impact that being happy in yourself can make on others. Seligman is one of the most prominent researchers in the field, often referred to as *the grandfather of positive psychology*. He was one of the initial psychologists who worked to shift the perspective of psychological research: from looking at what is wrong to reminding people to flourish instead. In his book, he talks about how emotions can be contagious.

He discusses a study that was done in Framingham, Massachusetts where over 5000 residents were surveyed for multiple health-related matters, some psychological. In the study, the address of each participant was known, and the study discovered the relevance of emotional contagion. "The closer someone lived to someone who was lonely, the lonelier the second individual felt. The same was true for depression" (Seligman, 2011). The most fascinating piece of this study? This finding applied to happiness as well. "Happiness was even more contagious than loneliness or depression and it worked across time" (Seligman, 2011).

Whatever emotion we experience impacts others around us. If *we* choose happiness, it's catching to those around us and it also spreads further.

The findings of this study are important for those who suffer from a guilty complex when working on their own happiness. When we nourish our own true happiness, not only do we impact ourselves, but also those around us. Therefore, when we bring happiness into our lives, we help others find happiness too, simply by helping to lift the mood of the environment. Let's face it: it's a lot easier to be happy when we are surrounded by smiling people versus those who complain, get angry or seem negative all the time.

The challenge is that guilt pervades. When we're not feeling happy, we can feel guilty for bringing others down! Yet feeling sad or angry can be the path to choosing happy. All those feelings are part of being human. If we don't allow ourselves to feel the full spectrum of human emotions, we numb our ability to feel at all, including our ability to feel happiness and positive emotions. More on this later.

The way to change our own happiness is to start with ourselves, not looking at others to make changes or do the work first. This can be a difficult lesson to digest but no one else is responsible for making you happy. No one can make you happy except you. You have to be willing to let happiness in and live. Can others make it easier or more difficult to experience happiness? Of course! But ultimately, your happiness lies in your hands. You are the one who has to begin.

Now, there are areas where we don't have choice. We don't get to decide how others experience or express their own happiness. We don't get to project the importance or value of happiness onto others because that would imply, we are in control of them. Making the choice to support them while still working on your own happiness is paramount. If you want happiness, then it's imperative to work with any fears that come with it, as well as embracing your own personal power of choice.

Just in case you needed a little more evidence for why allowing yourself to be happy doesn't mean you are selfish, have you ever heard of the feel-good-do-good syndrome? This is a particular phenomenon discussed in the world of psychology. I learned about it my first-year psych 101 course. In short, the feel-good-do-good syndrome is the idea that we are more likely to do good deeds when we feel good ourselves. That includes good deeds for other people and making good decisions. A behavioural pattern exists where the likelihood of us wanting to help others and making the world a better place increases if we are happy. This, I would argue, demonstrates a global benefit for your happiness. Being happy does not mean something 'bad' is waiting around the corner or that you are being selfish. Quite the opposite. If you contribute to your own happiness, you are more likely to go out into the world and create *another* good, helpful or happy scenario.

(Side note: helping others is a happiness strategy in itself. More detail later on.)

The interesting component of the anti-happiness arguments I've so far mentioned is they all rely on the idea that happiness exists outside of us. Quite the opposite is true. Real authentic happiness comes from within. Holocaust survivor and psychologist Viktor Frankl sums up the truest source of happiness in his book *Man's Search for Meaning*: "Even though conditions such as lack of sleep, insufficient food and various mental stresses may suggest that the inmates were bound to react in certain ways, in the final analysis, it becomes clear that the sort of person the prisoner became was the result of an inner decision, and not the result of camp influences alone. Fundamentally, therefore, any man can, even under such circumstances, decide what shall become of him-mentally and spiritually."

Often, we are convinced that we just need this much more money, a different boss or to move to a different place in order to be happy. Realistically speaking, all of these factors indeed play a role in our happiness, but not to the extent that many people believe.

According to University of California Riverside researcher Sonja Lyubomirsky, 10% of our happiness is based on circumstance. There is no denying that the environment we live in, the people we surround ourselves with, what is happening to the people we love and whether we are drowning in debt (and on and on) all have an impact on our happiness. However, that impact does not play as big a role as you might expect. An incredible 50% of our happiness is based on genetics. Indeed, a significant portion of our happiness exists at birth or is based on genetic disposition. We don't have much if any control over our genetic make-up. However, with the study of epigenetics, beliefs around the permanent impact of DNA are now being questioned. Epigenetics shows that certain genetic codes have tags that can be influenced by environmental factors, which can change how the gene is expressed. (*What?!* Epigenetics is mind-blowing.) This means a person and their physical and emotional habits and environment influence the aspect of the gene that expresses.

Nobel prize winner Elizabeth Blackburn's research demonstrates how mindful habits impact telomeres, which exist at the end of chromosomes. Telomeres act as a protective element for chromosomes. Over time, as telomeres break down, health-related issues such as cancer, cardiovascular disease and more, become an increased risk. However, research now shows that after three months of mindfulness practice, healthy eating and exercise, the once-believed-permanent damage to the telomeres, repairs. This research could challenge how much impact genetics plays in many areas, including its role in happiness. In regard to the happiness gene, there is currently not enough research to determine specific epigenetic tags. However, we must still be careful how much 'blame' we allow to land on genetics.

What we do know is that 40% of your happiness is based on intentional activities (Lyubomirsky). While lower than the genetic component, if I were to say to you that your income would increase by 40%, you would be convinced about the massive impact that would have on what you were able to purchase or do with your money. Likewise, if you had 40% more space in your house, that's a lot more space! Imagine taking advantage of that 40% and consistently applying the gift of choice – the gift of intentional activities – to support a happy life. I recognize that the genetic component will allow some people an excuse to dismiss their ability to choose happy, but that is their choice. Don't let it be yours! It is vital to process how big an impact our choices truly can make on our experience of life.

This book is filled with choices you can implement immediately that will have a massive impact on your happiness. I recommend applying them one at a time, rather than attempting all of them at once, which could overwhelm you and defeat the purpose of your attempt. One at a time is a much simpler and more effective approach.

Making the conscious choice to move down this path of choosing happy has opened up a life that I never would have believed was possible or available to me. We can't say for sure what the future will hold. However, if happiness is something you are open to, I can say from my own personal experiences and watching those of others, it will be there and may show up in the most unexpected ways. Does that mean life will be adversity-free? Nope. But it does mean, when you're willing to do the work and embrace your choices, happiness will always be there for the taking.

So back to 'other fear'. When the awareness of what you are afraid of surfaces, the next step is cultivating compassion and patience to make the necessary choices to create change and knowing that choosing happy is possible. Always. Some choices have an immediate impact, while others may take time. Some will require a really long time. And that's okay. There may be extra work or healing necessary before you can overcome your other fear. Throughout this book, we will look at some of that work and healing. What can you do to help move past other fear?

Besides using *The Many Sides of Happy* as your guide on this journey, you may also find it valuable to get in touch with a therapist or coach you trust to help you move past fear or at least work with it, so you can embrace your superpower of choosing happy.

PART ONE: HAPPINESS GROUNDWORK

The Happiness Groundwork Tools

If we want the outcome to be successful and sustainable, a solid foundation is necessary for pretty much anything, whether it's building a house, getting an education or living our lives safely. The same applies for creating and choosing a happy life.

To live happily, the place to start and consistently check into is our *intentional habits*. These are highly researched and documented actions that directly impact our happiness. I refer to these activities or habits is as the *happiness groundwork*.

Throughout my years of practicing and teaching happiness, these groundwork tools have proven effective. Initially, when I began my own choosing happy work, I chose to do these activities organically, almost intuitively, and sometimes out of sheer desperation. Later, I found out there was scientific evidence to back my experience. Personally, I have felt the shift that each one of these groundwork activities can make. I've also watched these actions make a difference for thousands of others.

Here is a brief introduction to your Happiness Groundwork Tools. The following chapters outline each element in greater detail.

Affirmations

Using affirmations, especially in the initial stages of working with choosing happy, is an incredibly simple and powerful tool that impacts happiness and overall wellbeing (Nelson, Fuller, Choi and Lyubomirsky, 2014). Affirmations can serve as the first line of defense when we're trying to make any kind of shift in our lives. When looking for more happiness, beginning each day with a positive affirmation will certainly initiate change.

Gratitude

Gratitude work is regularly demonstrated as a powerful tool for improving happiness in positive psychology research. It has even been demonstrated as a buffer against psychopathology (Petrocchi, N., and Couyoumdjian, A., 2015). If you find yourself in a funk, are struggling with choosing happy, or just want a regular daily activity packed with positivity, taking time out to reflect on what you are grateful for is a profoundly effective, simple and free activity to choose.

Diet

Numerous studies on food's impact on hormones indicate how our diet can make us unhappy. The converse is also true. There is copious research on how food sensitivities can cause symptoms of anxiety and depression to name a few (Naseribafrouei, A., 2014). Underlying lesson? Never underestimate the impact of what you eat on your happiness.

Journaling

Journaling is such a beneficial exercise for so many reasons, one of which being its positive impact on our happiness. Whether it's taking the time to pause and reflect daily, journal affirmations, journal gratitude or journal goals, research demonstrates that those doing the activity experience positive benefits (Frein and Ponsler, 2013) such as decreased stressed, greater clarity and focus, and an overall increase in feeling happy.

Exercise

Exercise — as in physical activity that gets your heart rate up and causes you to break into a sweat — is such an important tool with a multitude of purposes. Exercise impacts our health and behaves as a powerful prevention strategy for countless diseases. It is also crucial for choosing happy. I've experienced this in my own life, in my work with Choosing Happy workshops and coaching clients, and of course, the science backs this up too (Rasciute and Downward, 2010). Seriously, get out there and move your body! You will be well on your way to choosing happy.

Meditation

As more and more research shows, meditation is a powerful and beneficial daily practice for many reasons. Awareness of this is growing. One of those reasons is the profound impact it has on mood and increasing our ability to be happy.

Random Acts of Kindness

Kindness towards others is not only a mood-booster; it's also a lot of fun, and benefits individuals and communities as well as yourself.

Implementing these groundwork tools into my own life and with workshop participants has created lasting positive results. The cool part is more and more research is surfacing around the impact of these tools on happiness. Science demonstrates that each of these actions are incredibly valuable for choosing happy.

Understanding that there are multiple components for creating a solid foundation of happiness can be exciting yet overwhelming. There is an incredible amount of information you can take away on each of these tools. You could learn continuously about every one of the groundwork activities and never be finished. This is where it's important to take deep breaths and use your power of choice to pick just one. Start small, integrating one of these techniques into your daily life. Once that becomes a habit and no longer feels like an extreme effort, introduce the next. If you miss a day here or there, have compassion with yourself, recognizing it's a process not a destination and that you are continually, intentionally choosing happy.

Moving into the next section, I will discuss each of the Happiness Groundwork Tools in greater detail, how they impacted my own happiness journey and how you can begin to integrate them into your life.

As you may have guessed by the term 'groundwork', there is other further work involved in choosing true sustainable happiness. However, we start from the ground up. This is how we build a solid and reliable happiness foundation. This is also why I use the term 'choosing', because it is an ongoing process. That terminology is a reminder that happiness is in abundance and can't run out. It may disappear from our lenses at times, but it is always there when we are ready to connect. We can always be choosing. It's not a once-in-a-lifetime opportunity.

CHAPTER 3

Affirmations and Attention

The number of times I have said to myself, *well, I guess, I have no choice*, and felt completely powerless in whatever I faced, I couldn't even begin to count. For sure, I've felt I had to do what I didn't necessarily want to do. However, there still existed one place where I had a say in the matter... My reaction to the circumstances or situation. I could decide the narrative or dialogue that went on in my thoughts.

The internal statements we make at the start of each day are a choice we can all access. When I hit what I consider my 'rock bottom' during my dad's recovery, the only place I believed I could begin to access was in my mind, my thoughts. I could change what I was thinking when I woke up and heard him walking down the hall. Before I figured out to shout *"I am happy"* in my head, terrible thoughts would run through my mind. Thoughts of anger and resentment. Statements like: "what's the point?" or "get ready for another reminder of the shit-show you call life."

This way of thinking would set me up to be receptive to all the challenging, disappointing and sad circumstances that were going on. Those thoughts would close my ability to receive or even see any of the good. Indeed, hard stuff was going on. However, there were also amazing opportunities and friendships in my life. I knew I wanted to feel the good too, so intuitively I began repeating what I now know to be an affirmation: "I am happy."

In order to create a shift from feeling trapped by my circumstances to something better, I felt the words "I am happy" were the easiest and most effective to take me towards what I wanted. At the time, these words felt like my *only* option. Otherwise, my thoughts would spiral into a state of grief and gloom. This was my introduction to the power and impact of affirmations; they changed my feelings and perspective on life.

Affirmations seem to be a common conversation now compared to when I began my "I am happy" morning routine. Approximately 10 years later, when I started hosting my Choosing Happy workshops, I did further research on affirmations. Having experienced their potency for myself, I wanted to see if their use was supported by anyone else. I quickly learned that affirmations were a popular tool used in the self-help community.

The dictionary definition of an affirmation is as follows:

1. *the act of affirming; state of being affirmed.*
2. *the assertion that something exists or is true.*
3. *something that is affirmed or declared to be true.*
4. *confirmation or ratification of a prior judgment, decision, etc.*
5. *solemn declaration accepted instead of a statement under oath.*

(Random House Kernerman Webster's College Dictionary, 2010)

First and foremost, an affirmation is a statement. It's important to understand affirmations can be positive or negative. When using affirmations, a particular statement is chosen that reinforces whatever outcome you are seeking. Looking at the fourth dictionary definition, it states "confirmation or ratification of a prior judgment or decision." In applying that to happiness, we are either using the affirmation to reinforce our current happy state or to get rid of our belief in an only-negative experience. Affirmations have the power to shift or reinforce our perspective.

According to many experts on the subject, affirmations should start with an "I am..." statement to be effective. Likewise, they must frame the outcome in such a way that it seems it is already happening. Using my example "I am happy," in the moment I used that statement, I didn't *actually* feel happy. Not even close. However, I did wholeheartedly believe that I had the ability to be truly happy, so it didn't feel as if I was being fake.

It is important to believe in the affirmation, understanding that the feeling of happiness may not be there just yet, but is absolutely available to you and may require just a little effort. Stating the "I am happy" affirmation almost felt like I was participating in a little scavenger hunt. I knew there was a treasure chest (AKA happiness) and I never doubted that happiness was possible, but I needed to go on this little journey to find it again. I fully recognized there would be bumps in the road. Heck, I felt like I was overcoming the Everest of grief when I started this process. I embraced that there would be circumstances where I wouldn't understand the clues. I knew there would be moments when I would be convinced that this happiness treasure chest was all in my imagination, because of the intense circumstances in my external environment. However, the "I am happy" affirmation behaved as a map, a reminder or a guide that would indeed help me find my happy treasure if only I kept it as my intention in the frontal cortex of my brain.

To be clear, affirmations are *only* the beginning. When it comes to experiencing lasting, fulfilling happiness, there is much more work and action that also needs to take place. Repeating affirmations over and over is one of the beginning pieces of that work, part of the groundwork, as they help to inspire, motivate, focus attention and support the efforts that will be required.

A study from University of California, Riverside and Seoul National University, South Korea tells us that affirmations have an impact on two 'types' of happiness:

Hedonic (Subjective Wellbeing)

Presence of positive mood
Absence of negative mood
Satisfaction with various domains of life (e.g. work, leisure)
Global life satisfaction

Eudaimonic (Psychological Wellbeing)

Sense of control or autonomy
Feeling of meaning and purpose
Personal expressiveness
Feelings of belongingness
Social contribution
Competence
Personal growth
Self-acceptance

When I began working with my "I am happy" affirmation, of course, I didn't analyze what 'type' of happiness I was hoping to impact. I was simply looking for something that was healthy and sustainable that could give me a sense that I would feel better at some point in the future. However, this information is valuable as it reinforces the impact a few simple positive words can make in many areas where we struggle or feel a sense of lack.

How Affirmations Work

When working toward choosing happy, it is crucial that the chosen affirmation is a positive one. Otherwise, the negative state you experience currently will be reinforced, thereby doing the opposite of creating happiness. One of the most influential experts in affirmation work is author and self-help publisher Louise Hay, whom I found many years into my journey. I was already a firm believer in saying my little internal mantra. Yet, it was Hay's work that truly brought me an understanding of what I was doing and where else in my life affirmations could play a role in happiness. It's not only the statement "I am happy" that impacts happiness but expanding this statement to other aspects that play into happiness. Whether it's success, healing, creativity, you name it, as Hay puts it, "An affirmation opens the door."

Action time:

Close your eyes and take three deep breaths. Once you've completed the third breath, pause and write three positive affirmations that you can connect with, that you are willing to say over and over each morning and throughout the day to begin your potential shift.

Here are a couple of suggestions to get you started. You are completely free to use these affirmations or take them as a starting point and design your own that are more meaningful and impactful for you. Sometimes talking your affirmations out with a trusted close friend can help you gain clarity on which ones you connect with. Then let go of others that don't offer the same holding power.

> "I am worthy of the happy life I say I want."
> "I am supported in my choices for health, healing and happiness."
> "I believe in my strengths and gifts, and use them to foster more happiness."
> "I am open to receive positivity and love in my life."
> "I am light, I am peace, I am love, I am happy."

Simply stating an affirmation over and over doesn't necessarily guarantee the affirmation will take hold. There are a few other elements. When implemented, these will reinforce the affirmation giving it that much more influential power. Here's how you can make your affirmations even more successful.

Constant Reminders

Writing the affirmation out on a piece of paper and posting it on your mirror, in your car or as the background screen on your phone can help to keep it in the forefront of your thoughts. The more repetition you have with your affirmations, the more they remain in the direct line of your attention. This can influence your behavior and choices. As James Redfield states, "Where the attention goes the energy flows." If you keep your focus on a particular affirmation, you are more likely to make choices in line with what you are affirming. The more often you make choices that reinforce the "I am happy" affirmation, the more happiness you will access.

Repeat During Physical Activity

I have used this technique regularly in workshops, exercise therapy sessions, yoga practices and on myself. It is an extremely powerful experience, where profound clarity comes from working with the body. Taking the affirmation through a somatic experience can offer a deeper level of integration. Throughout this book, you will see the repetition of the argument that the mind influences the body and the body influences the mind. This certainly applies to affirmations.

Whether on a run, going for a walk or practicing yoga, repeating an affirmation so the words can translate and land in your body creates an incredible impact. This allows you to connect to the 'gut response', also known as intuition or inner wisdom. Moving your body while repeating any affirmation allows that statement to land in a different way; it creates an experience where you not only *think* about the affirmation, but you *feel* it.

Let's face it: emotion overrides logic pretty much the majority of the time. Our bodies are powerful foundations for health and wellbeing. Therefore, bringing the affirmation into the body helps create a more solid foundation for the affirmation to take hold.

We also receive feedback on the statement, not just from a cognitive place but from a visceral one. Feedback may tell us that a particular affirmation makes sense for us or may indicate that it does not. If we find ourselves physically rejecting the affirmation, it could be for one of two reasons. Maybe we need to rephrase the affirmation because that language isn't working for us. Alternatively, we must embrace the fear that sometimes comes along with the idea of getting what we really want.

Be Patient and Open

Sometimes healing needs to happen before an affirmation can take hold and manifest itself into your reality. When in a dark place of suffering or frustration and seeking out happiness, you may be desperate for instant gratification.

It is important to stay open to what other information may be surfacing when trying to connect with an affirmation. If you notice a sense of anger or jealousy perhaps, then an affirmation to shift and heal might be required before being able to connect with your happiness intention.

Suggested Affirmations for Healing:

"I hold space for the uniqueness of my process."
"I am open to the love and support of others on my journey to happiness."
"I understand that growth, learning and healing take time."
"I support myself with patience and compassion."

Pay Attention to Your Attention

We all have a specific attention span, meaning we hold only a specific amount space in our minds to process only a specific amount of information at one time. If we only pay attention to what is going wrong in our lives, we don't have enough brain capacity to also witness the beauty around us. Therefore, in a short period of time, our brains can be convinced that life is only filled with tragedy, horror and sadness.

Now, there is no denying that life does have its challenges and severe traumas. However, life *also* has a lot of incredible things to offer as well. If happiness is something we are looking to have more of in our lives, then it is extremely important to take inventory of what we are paying attention to on a daily basis.

What we allow ourselves to pay attention to plays a *massive* role in our ability to choose happy. Dr. Mihaly Csikszentmihalyi, author of the national bestseller *Flow*, is a prominent researcher in the field of positive psychology. He discusses the powerful impact of how allocating our attention changes our ability to experience happiness, or as he calls it 'flow', meaning a happy state of mind. Csikszentmihalyi states, "Attention is like energy in that without it no work can be done and in doing work it is dissipated. We create ourselves by how we invest this energy. Memories, thoughts, and feelings are all shaped by how we use it. And it is energy under our control, to do with as we please; hence, attention is our most important tool in the task of improving the quality of experience" (Csikszentmihalyi, 1990).

When your happiness is being negatively impacted over an extended period of time, take a step back and start to watch what fills your day. Do you wake up and turn on social media or the News channel straight away, looking for the latest terror attack or horrible politicians in every election? Are you watching and waiting for someone to cut you off in traffic or to look at you the wrong way? Do you allow your brain to run off on some kind of judgmental rant along the lines of: *What are you looking at? Do you think there's something wrong with me? Do you think I'm ugly? Is there a problem with what I'm wearing? See that's what's wrong with the world...?*

The insanity in our brains can literally go on for a lifetime, take over our scope of attention and make us incredibly *unhappy*. If these types of thoughts are rushing in or taking over, you need to take serious action. The good news is: you can!

I remember being angry and jealous of friends who had both parents still alive and supporting them through their university careers. So many people said these were the best days of my life and I wanted to punch them in the face! I had a pretty powerful story running through my head reinforcing all of these reasons I was unhappy. Bizarrely, there even came a point where I almost felt *entitled* to my unhappiness. That didn't serve me at all; while I sure had reasons to be unhappy, thinking that way didn't do me any good. Thinking that way left me in more of an unwanted state: deeply unhappy. I am so grateful I found a way to shift my attention.

Being aware of the power of our attention is a valuable place to start. However, it's also about holding ourselves accountable for where we allocate it.

Action time:

Go into observation mode for a day.
   Look for people smiling, people holding doors, flowers, trees, people laughing, people dancing, people having a nice time with their friends, children enjoying themselves, dogs playing. When you notice negative thoughts or judgments, yell the word 'stop' in your brain. (You could even yell it out loud. That might be a fun social experiment!)
   You may find you have days where you honestly hear yourself yelling 'stop' over 1,000 times. However, over time, this will shift and you will begin to notice the positivity, the simple little things.

Focus and Mindfulness

I had the privilege of running multiple 30-day challenges at the yoga studio where I worked. At the beginning of each challenge, we would have a theme and ask our participants to set a goal to reinforce that theme, then see what came of it over the next 30 days. During one particular challenge, we had a participant who absolutely *loved* watching TV. It was her favorite downtime activity. She genuinely wanted to challenge herself and knew that giving up watching TV for the 30 days would throw her headfirst into this challenge. She held up to her goal and the shift it created in her life was greater than she could've ever possibly imagined. At first, it was hard for her to not watch TV, because it was an escape that she thoroughly enjoyed. However, as time went on, she was exposed to so many other activities that brought her pleasure and joy. She began to see the world and what it had to offer through a different lens. She would recount to us over and over how much she found in her life to be grateful for but had simply never noticed when she was so distracted watching TV. This participant went on to get into meditation and found an entirely new world for herself. She found so much joy and healing in meditation that she became a meditation teacher.
   I don't share this story to convince you that you have to stop watching TV and become a meditation teacher in order to shift your perspective. I share this story because sometimes we need to step outside of ourselves and shift our focus to realize what we have access to is right at our fingertips. Nothing changed monetarily in this person's life; no crazy miraculous events happened that rendered her happy all of a sudden. She shifted the allocation of her attention intentionally

and found her happy. Indeed, when we hold ourselves accountable for what fills our attention, we can change our lives in a dramatic fashion.

We need to be extremely aware of how we fill our time and thoughts. It could be television, technology, career, gossip… the list goes on and on. If what you are paying attention to is making you feel yucky, drained, exhausted or negative, it's time to see if there is space to make some changes and allow yourself to experience what makes you feel good.

A powerful practice that involves allocating our attention into the present moment is *mindfulness*. I once attended a full-day mindfulness conference with Dr. Dan Siegel, an expert in the field of mindfulness. He described mindfulness as "focused attention from a place of compassion." I like that definition, especially the compassion part. As you're working through this book, be sure to honour your efforts from a place of compassion.

IMPORTANT: There are copious mindfulness techniques used to help people experiencing depression, anxiety and other mental health disorders. Addressing these and other mood disorders is beyond the scope of this book and this conversation. The suggestions in this book may be beneficial to add in combination with the advice and prescribed treatment of your mental health professional and are not intended as a substitute.

I began practicing mindfulness when I was dealing with my dad's heart attack and attending university. At the time, I didn't have a name for what I was doing, and no one had told me this was what I should do. I almost fell upon this mental practice and discovered it helped me feel good.

My mindfulness technique revolved entirely around my meals, in particular, my lunch. To be honest, my university lunches were nothing to write home about. Most days they were packed in whatever plastic grocery bag I could find and consisted of cheese and crackers on the side of an MSG-filled packet soup that I would mix with boiling water in my stainless-steel mug.

DISCLAIMER! As a health practitioner and someone who fully understands how quality of food impacts your happiness, this is not a diet I would recommend!

Nonetheless, each day at lunch, I would have this sense of excitement. I would get to sit down with my favorite mug, eat my sodium-filled soup, and enjoy some crackers and cheese. I would even tell my friends how excited I was for lunch each and every day. Here's why: in that moment, I would pause and taste every single bite. I would hold my mug and feel the warmth. I would chew slowly and savour the food. I would sit among my friends having conversations about our dreams and next steps. I would be so immersed in that moment, tasting every different flavor (admittedly not much!) and hearing the voices of my friends.

It was a minute of magic to me, a pause when I wasn't worrying about my dad, wasn't drowning in my own grief. Those simple moments were a breath of fresh air. They made me feel alive.

None of this changed what was happening at home with my dad, none of this changed my debt-filled finances. Yet in those moments, I had the ability to feel bliss. The key was just fully showing up.

Being mindful and disciplined to stay connected to joyful moments is a powerful secret in the art of choosing happy. I had to be willing to sit down, willing to open my eyes and look at this mug, willing to allow my friends to be around me and then open enough to let the moment in.

Like I said, I didn't realize I was practicing *mindfulness*. At least, not by that name. Now it has become a daily practice throughout my life. I give myself permission to be as present as possible to everything that brings me joy and fills my cup. I also stay as present as possible in the uncomfortable moments. One can be a happy reminder; the other can be a powerful teacher and opportunity for growth. Even if it is only for a brief moment, I make a conscious effort to include a mindful act at some point.

Action time:

Write down three activities where you could allow yourself to be more mindful. Some suggestions:

> *When out for a walk, take in the trees and count the branches. Look for flowers.*
>
> *If with family, actively listen to what they are saying. Let go of the urge to respond or cut in.*
>
> *At dinner, count the number of times you chew. Pause and focus on each flavor you taste in your food.*
>
> *When lying in bed about to go to sleep, notice each inhale and exhale of your breath. Count how many breaths you watch before you find*

yourself focusing on something else. Then of course, when you realize you're thinking of something else, come back to counting your breath.

Create a gratitude journal. Each day write down five things you are grateful for and why you are grateful. Connecting with why you are grateful will draw your attention even deeper to the things that make you feel good.

There are numerous apps and websites that are fully dedicated to mindfulness. I highly recommend checking them out and making mindfulness a priority in your daily routine.

And watch how your happiness grows.

CHAPTER 4

Let's Get Physical

To get straight to the point here: exercise is an *absolute non-negotiable* to setting the foundation for happiness and living a healthy life. What's fantastic about exercise is it's something you can *choose* to do at any point in time. The catch is not everyone *wants* to make that choice!

If you are already exercising, fantastic! Use this chapter as a little extra motivation to keep doing what you're doing. As well, you can take advantage of the workout included in the appendix as another option.

If you aren't exercising, I do understand it can be difficult to begin, but it's not impossible, especially when you examine why you're resisting. The resistance that surfaces around this particular subject is fascinating. Numerous times when I've been presenting on choosing happy and brought up the importance of exercise, I've heard feedback like: "when you talk about the exercise part, you make me feel guilty, because I think about doing it but then don't" or "I already know about the importance of exercise and I don't want to hear about it again, so tell me something else."

This is one of those situations where we have to give ourselves a huge reality check. I acknowledge that some people have physical limitations on the type of exercise they can do. However, if you are looking for inspiration from someone who moves far beyond his physical limitations, check out Zach Anner and his incredible Workout Wednesday videos. Anner has cerebral palsy and spends a significant amount of his time in a wheelchair but doesn't allow that to stop him from getting his exercise on or the unbelievable motivation he provides to the world. He makes a choice. It's not an easy choice, but he still recognizes that he has one.

The Many Sides of Happy

When it comes to choosing happy, especially in the beginning, making choices that will ultimately render you authentically happy may not be easy. I get it. People are busy, working crazy hours, raising children, doing their thing. However, if you would describe yourself as an unhappy person who wants to live a happy life and are not a regular exerciser, you have to get serious with yourself and use your ability to choose exercise. You can choose to start at any time.

When I worked in the fitness industry, I met so many people who came into the gym having never worked out in their life. There was one particular guy who was a smoker, borderline obese, newly divorced and unbelievably grumpy. Let's call him Fred for privacy purposes. He was an extremely busy entrepreneur who had resting angry face and was recovering from back surgery. Exercise for him was excruciatingly difficult. In the beginning, everything felt inconvenient and hard. Frankly, he hated it.

Fred's workout began with simply moving in any way. After about three months, shifts crept in. Fred became a bit stronger. He quit smoking, lost a significant amount of weight and worked out every single day. Even his resting angry face softened! He actually smiled sometimes! He found within him the energy, discipline and ability to choose. He persevered. Everyone in the gym was shocked at the profound physical as well as behavioral changes that took place.

I know firsthand that when I'm not exercising regularly the shift in my mood can be extreme. Any ability to look on the bright side diminishes dramatically. Of course, the opposite occurs when I exercise regularly. After a good workout, my mood is lighter, tasks I found irritating or overwhelming become so much more manageable.

The situation with my dad's heart attack during my time at university was stressful. Having a built-in coping mechanism (a degree in exercise science) was extremely helpful. On top of the course work, in order to graduate, we had to participate in a certain number of practicums. That year, I was taking swimming and yoga; their impact on my ability to process the stress I was experiencing was immeasurable. This exercise made it a lot easier to connect with my "I am happy" affirmations.

When it comes to affirmations, the statement plants a seed, then the aligned actions you take create the manifestation. Whenever I exercised, it was guaranteed that I would come out feeling better than I felt before. Anything that could help alleviate the heaviness of my dad's circumstances felt like magic. Exercise became almost a portal that transported me to a place where happiness and feeling good were still available for me to experience, even amongst the chaos. Best described, it gave me *relief* from the emotional pain. And I needed that relief desperately after reliving my mother's death over and over and watching the father I knew growing up disappear in front of my eyes. I do not have enough words in my vocabulary to describe that pain.

    Now, exercise is not the only technique I could have used to provide a sense of relief and create a sense of pleasure. Some people turn elsewhere. Drugs and alcohol can provide that instant pick-me-up and a temporary sense of pleasure that some would describe as happiness. However, these substances create an illusion of happiness that is fleeting. This type of 'bliss' is not choosing happy. It is avoiding pain. And there's a big difference. Later in this book, I discuss the importance of leaning into pain in order to have true authentic happiness. This choosing happy groundwork lays the foundation to make leaning in possible.

    Drugs, alcohol, excessive spending through gambling or shopping and many other pain-avoiding behaviours can create significant damage that can lead to the exact opposite of happiness. When making choices to create a happy life for ourselves, it's extremely important to view whatever we are doing with our minds or our bodies from a place of love and kindness. Harming our health is not treating ourselves with love and kindness. It may be feeding a pleasure principle. However, it's not choosing happy. The occasional glass of wine or retail therapy, that is a different story. When a behaviour becomes a habit of consistently avoiding pain, then it is no longer choosing happy, no longer truly living.

    To facilitate your happiness and own the fact you have choice, you have to get real with yourself and recognize a certain amount of personal discipline will be required. Yeah, I know I said the D-word. I get that the word 'discipline' isn't usually associated with fun or joy. However, discipline is a must for creating your happiest life.

    Exercise is one of those things that many (including me) resist because, when we first take it up, it can be uncomfortable, awkward and challenging. I have had many clients reiterate, in a few choice words I might add, that their workout feels like the furthest feeling from happiness. However, when they are finished their workout, they feel that sense of accomplishment and experience the workout high.

The Science Proves It

Don't just take my word for it. There is copious amounts of research demonstrating the positive impact that exercise has on our happiness.

That post-exercise happy boost comes when we endure a certain length of exercise because our bodies release endorphins, also known as happy hormones (Rasciute and Downward, 2010). Interestingly, endorphins don't actually make us feel happy. Endorphins increase our tolerance to pain and discomfort. When we are more tolerant to discomfort, it's a lot easier to gather perspective and choose happy.

What's more: if we work for our bodies, our bodies will work for us. They will give back and contribute to the happy work. When we have more of these happy hormones running through our bodies, we *feel* good, meaning it will take less mental work to say to ourselves "I am happy." We are doing intentional activity to support that initial affirmation. Physical activity helps to decrease the size of the mental hurdle we sometimes have to overcome to connect with the thoughts and experiences of being happy.

Once this physical feel-good experience happens, a ripple effect can occur. We feel good so we have an easier time focusing on good thoughts and circumstances. The more we focus on the good, the more we fill our attention with positivity. The more we fill our attention with positivity, the more we enter into the sense of *flow*, which we learned earlier is that happy mindset.

No matter who I work with – individual clients, group classes or workshop participants – the response is unanimous 99% of the time: everyone feels better after a workout.

Next up: another happy hormone. When we exercise, dopamine is released and can stay in our system up to 48 hours after the initial activity. That means after you participate in some kind of challenging exercise, you get a two-day feel-good boost. The sustained happiness provided by exercise is higher than the happiness provided by sugar. When we eat sugar, we experience a sugar rush that can feel fantastic, but shortly after, it is followed by the sugar crash, which depletes us further from the baseline where we began before we ate it. Not exercise though! Exercise is the gift that keeps on giving.

Interestingly, research finds unique exercise increases dopamine release. Something as simple as changing your walking route can count as 'unique'. If you participate in group exercise or yoga, simply varying your usual spot in the classroom can create an increased happy hormone release.

Benefits of exercise are numerous, from helping to treat anxiety and depression to decreasing risk of sickness through boosted immunity, increasing the ability to focus and slowing down the aging process (Dishman et al, 2012). The list for why we should exercise goes on and on, and while I'll repeatedly argue the extreme importance of moving your body, I understand not everyone is into boot camps or marathons. Fortunately, it doesn't take an insanely intense level of exercise to create a happy hormone release. Some studies show that endorphin release can happen in as little as 10 minutes of intense physical activity. Others show it can take 20 to 30 minutes of more moderate intensity exercise. Liberally speaking, in approximately 30 minutes of movement, everyone has the power to create a physical foundation to support happiness.

No exercise regime should break the bank either. The point is to make the choice to do it, so we need to remove those barriers. If joining a gym or a studio interests you, make sure the costs work within your budget. Happy-inducing exercise doesn't need to cost a dime. While you should speak with your doctor before starting any kind of exercise regimen or program, anyone (who is physically able) can get up and go for a walk, either outside or up and down the stairs in their building.

From an unhappy place, we tend to overcomplicate or overthink exercise, because we are aching for that sense of relief. At some point, we have to make a decision as to what is important. Those thoughts and excuses around not having enough time, energy or money can keep us stuck. If you hear those convincing little voices in your head, remember the mindfulness groundwork from the last section. Yell *"stop"* in your mind and then just begin your exercise, let me repeat, just begin. Start to move your body for an extended period, then tap into the way you *feel*.

Happiness is a Feeling

Happiness is not something you analyze or some kind of logical formula. Happiness requires us to be open to *feeling*. When starting to exercise, for the purpose of connecting to happiness, choose to do whatever movement you enjoy. It's not about choosing the latest greatest fad that's 'guaranteed' to give you the specific body type you may seek. Move your body in ways that give you a sense of lightness inside.

The positive feedback of connecting with something that makes you feel good is what will keep you going back for more. It's sustainable. Whenever I began training with a new client, the first couple of workouts would all just be about getting their bodies moving and creating an experience where they simply felt good. Yes, many of them would attest that their workouts became more challenging as time went on. However, that depended on their goals at the time. Clients who were dealing with chronic illness such as fibromyalgia, Parkinson's disease or cancer were not working out for the greatest looking body. They were using exercise strategically to create a feel-good feedback system and sense of internal strength, the emotional boost to want to face another day. Depending on the disease and the circumstances, I've used exercise as a powerful aspect of treatment for some of these diseases with my clients. Many were able to decrease the amount of medication they were taking. Some were able to get off medication altogether and felt better. This was incredible considering the negative emotional impact of some medication side effects.

At this point, I must emphasise that I am not suggesting that everyone drop all pharmaceuticals and only pump iron at the gym. This process needs to be supervised by both the physician and a qualified fitness professional trained in exercise therapy, because when we begin to exercise, many of the body's systems have to adapt and readjust to what we are asking it to do.

The nervous system is one such component. Going from zero to 100 when beginning to exercise can create an uncomfortable experience as the body hasn't had time to adjust. You have to condition your nervous system to learn how to fire and how to recruit your muscles in the right way for what you're asking your body to do.

Likewise, let me make it extremely clear that I'm also definitely not saying you should never push yourself, because working out hard can create immense benefits. Facing challenges and overcoming them is an exceptional way of raising the bar when it comes to happiness. I am a huge advocate of setting of goals, working hard and pushing through obstacles to achieve them. As with anything new though, you have to find the space that allows you to just begin. There is a process that needs to happen to allow your body to change in a healthy way so you can continue to exercise and feel good. If you do too much exercise too soon at the beginning, you can experience negative side effects or even injury, which can set you back further maybe limiting your ability to exercise.

So where do you begin?

Action time:

It's time stop thinking and reading about exercise and... actually get physical!

    Below you will find a list of suggestions to choose from. This list is not comprehensive, but a collection of ideas sent to me by a wide variety of friends and colleagues when I asked them to share physical activity they enjoyed. The activities are not in a specific order, simply in the order I received them. There's plenty more you may want to try. Feel free to add any that I haven't included here.

    Take a moment and scan the list of activities for ideas you either know you love or somewhat pique your interest. Maybe there are only a few items on the list below that you kind of like or are perhaps willing to do. Hey, if something only slightly interests you, but nothing else really jumps out, no worries. Just pick that and give it a try. Some of us will feel passionate and drawn to particular activities, where others may be only slightly interested. Either way, choose at least three activities or choose one activity you are willing to do at least three times, and write it down.

    Next, set some dates where you will go out and *do the activity*.

    Finally, make it your mission to complete all three of your top feel-good physical activities by the end of the month (or do your one top feel-good activity three times). Realistically though, you want to work up to the point where you are moving your body nearly every day.

    Recognize that the one activity you may want to do more than anything might not be in season or in your price range. If that is the case, do not let this be a reason to avoid this exercise. Choose something else and stick to your goal of getting active.

    Here is a list of physical activity suggestions I received from my social media survey. When asked what physical activity made them feel happy, people said:

- *yoga*
- *grooming a horse*
- *horseback riding*
- *hiking in the woods*
- *walking in nature*
- *gardening*
- *running*
- *paddling on water*

- *kayaking*
- *canoeing*
- *HIIT (high intensity interval training)*
- *rock-climbing*
- *Zumba*
- *tennis*
- *walking in sunshine*
- *tai chi*
- *karate*
- *SUP (stand-up paddleboarding)*
- *snowboarding*
- *dancing*
- *surfing*
- *playing basketball*
- *golf*
- *skiing*
- *snorkeling*
- *pilates*
- *soccer*
- *roller-blading*
- *curling*
- *washing the car*
- *sex*
- *volleyball*
- *qi-gung*
- *spinning*
- *step classes*
- *skating*
- *swimming.*

A number of the responses mentioned the musical and social aspects of doing physical activities. So, have a great playlist and move your body with your favorite people.

Finally, as you begin your activity of choice, remember your "I am happy" affirmation. Repeat your affirmation periodically throughout the physical activity, allowing your positive statement to land on a more visceral level.

See Appendix A for the 20-minute Happy Workout or Appendix B for the 20-minute Happy Yoga Practice

Flourish!

There is a direct correlation between physical activity and flourishing mental health. If the guidelines above do not mirror (are less) then the current amount of physical activity you are getting each week, there will absolutely be an impact on your experience of happiness. I cannot emphasize enough that getting active is a choice. It's an option that is always available and does not have to cost a lot. There may be many obstacles you have to face or heal to find your happy. However, getting physically active is so profound and effective in helping you along the way and the evidence supporting this is staggering.

You can do this!

There are so many free resources at your local library, online, at community centers and so on. Even big corporations such as Lululemon and Lolë have free programs for the community to help make physical activity more accessible. If you are hesitating in any way, please remind yourself you deserve to be your happiest and healthiest self. Giving yourself the gift of physical activity is one of the greatest happiness tools out there.

Go get active now! Choosing to get active is choosing happy. And it's a choice you have.

CHAPTER 5

MMMMMM FOOOOD!

We can't talk about the groundwork of choosing happy without addressing the extent to which food impacts our happiness. Of course, nutrition is a vast subject; to narrow it down to one chapter is impossible. However, since the quality of your food, food sensitivities, and digestive system function all have a massive – I mean *massive* – impact on your mood and ability to choose happiness, it must be included in this book.

Clients' reactions to the suggestion that they change their diet are similar to their reactions when I suggest exercise. That is: not overly enthusiastic. Making the best nutrition choices to support our happiest lives requires effort, time and knowledge. Just like exercise, in the beginning, making changes in our diets can seem overwhelming and intimidating. As someone who has had more kitchen accidents and near-fires than I would like to admit, I fully understand how daunting it is to think about cooking more, planning meals and cutting out some of those foods we *think* are pleasurable.

However, what you put in your body will impact your brain function, energy levels, mood fluctuations and immunity. Having good supportive fuel in your body creates an invaluable energy reserve that you will need to draw on when you are confronted with happiness-related choices.

I am reminded of the impact of food with my own family. My eldest son suffers from asthma. Removing dairy from his diet had a huge impact on his health. When you can breathe properly, it's a lot easier to access happiness. When I had cancer, I shifted my diet significantly and was able to leave the hospital from my second surgery in three days instead of six, and lift weight again in six weeks instead of eight. I was also blessed with not having to go through further treatment. My doctor and surgeon were shocked by the outcome. They told me my healthy lifestyle habits were a major contributor, but they believed my positive attitude had the biggest impact.

These examples showed me the importance of food, but my husband Ed's experience was most potent in understanding the value of knowing food sensitivities and eating well. He suffered from major migraines and – somewhat scarily – was demonstrating stroke symptoms such as slurred speech and confusion. Ed also experienced brutal stomach pain and was rushed to the hospital with excruciating heart pain on a number of occasions. He started to withdraw from life. His sense of humor diminished and his overall zest for life was disappearing. His sense of humor and love of life are the things I love most about Ed, so when these began to fade, we knew something was seriously up.

Ed wanted to do something. To say he went through a crazy amount of medical tests would be an understatement. MRI scanning, echo-stress testing, neurological testing, multiple rounds of bloodwork, ultrasounds to name a few. Every test he took came back as 'normal' except his bloodwork, which showed issues with his thyroid. The doctor explained that my husband would need to go on medication for the rest of his life. He asked our doctor if it was possible for him to try diet modifications over the next few months to see if this could make an impact. She told us the likelihood was slim, but would entertain the idea and redo his bloodwork in a couple of months; if there was no change, medication would be the only option.

My husband did a full-on shift in his diet, including cutting out gluten. We didn't know for sure that he was gluten-sensitive, but we were fortunate to have friends who are experts in nutrition and gave us this recommendation. The changes he experienced did not happen immediately. It required patience and a leap of faith. Fortunately, he knew this wasn't about the quick fix; it was about his long-term health and happiness. As each week passed, the symptoms he had been experiencing began to diminish: headaches less frequent, clarity where he had once experienced brain fog, increased energy levels, an ability to be present and have fun.

Finally, he went back to the doctor after three months of adhering to a gluten-free lifestyle to have his blood taken again. In the doctor's words, the results were 'shocking'. She had never seen thyroid numbers shift so much without the support of medication. It was simply mind-blowing to her, so much so that she decided to do her own research on the impacts a gluten-free diet can make for those who are suffering with thyroid issues.

I would love to say that Ed is 100% better since he changed his diet, but he isn't. However, he has come a long, long way and the foundation of food has played a significant role in his improvements. He is a firm believer that his mindset and stress management are the biggest players in terms of his health. And when his diet is healthier, his ability to manage his mindset and choose happy is much improved.

Thus, we discuss the importance of a healthy diet as a Happiness Groundwork Tool...

Finding Your Unique Formula

Here's the catch... There isn't one specific diet protocol that is best for everybody. Whether it's diet, exercise, your career path or your definition of happiness, we all have an individual formula that is the best approach for us.

For example, my husband went on a strict AIP (autoimmune protocol) diet and lost so much weight it was considerably unhealthy for him. The diet worsened the anxiety he was experiencing. His energy levels were dramatically impacted as well as his mental health. However, for some, this diet works incredibly well. For Ed to thrive, it involves eating a little bit of everything, by which I mean whole real foods (except those with gluten), not bags of chips and chocolate bars, and not being super rigid. For others to thrive, it will look different.

The takeaway lesson here is you need to respect yourself and your body enough to figure out what foods and eating times make you feel your best.

So, where do you even begin?

Trying to figure out what is best to eat can be one hell of a nightmare. In this chapter, I give some simple, foundational suggestions. Alongside this information, I would highly recommend seeing a holistic nutritionist, following nutritionists on social media, heading to your local library to educate yourself or even taking a course. This is your body and your life. Your health and nutrition matter. You matter!

For a beginner approach to eating well for happiness, my recommendation is simple: eat a majority plant-based diet made up of lots of water, whole organic unprocessed fruits and vegetables, healthy fats, local organic meats and wild-caught fish. Basing most meals on this suggestion will support your body for your happiness quest in a powerful way. Eating well balances hormones, creates sustainable energy, boosts mood, helps with sleep, impacts the healing process of tissues in the body, impacts gut bacteria, and so much more. The impact of food consumption on mental health is profound and key groundwork for choosing happy.

An interesting fact on gut bacteria: research demonstrates a significant link between gut bacteria and depression (Naseribafrouei, A., 2014).

There are a number of roadblocks that might prevent you feeling like making any changes. Stay with me, because now we're going to cover some of the common issues that get in the way when we try to make dietary changes.

"I have changed my eating habits but not feeling any improvements..."

If you find yourself no closer to choosing happy after making dietary changes, going for a food sensitivity test could help you figure out what foods may be aggravating your system.

It's amazing when you feel the difference by eliminating foods that — while tasty — are wreaking havoc on the inside. For me, cutting out dairy was a game-changer. For others, it may make no difference. Trial and error will be required here, but when you begin to address your diet, you set off on a beneficial path towards happiness.

Other than seeking out the advice of a nutritionist, you could go to your local health food store or take out a book on nutrition from the library to give you more knowledge. It is so valuable to educate yourself on what food choices will support you best.

"I hate cooking..."

For those who hate being in the kitchen, holy cow do I hear you! I am right there with you. Asking you to spend more time in the kitchen may feel like the exact opposite of choosing happy for you. I so get it. Here's the thing. Choosing happy is about the long-term game, not just the short-term fix. Sometimes we have to invest our time in some less favourable activities because it serves a greater purpose. Unless you're one of the lucky ones who loves it, cooking is one of those times.

Understanding *why* you're in the kitchen can be a wonderful mindset tool for this. I've always valued healthy eating. However, when different health scenarios presented themselves in our family — like my son's asthma, my cancer diagnosis, and my husband's digestive and mental health struggles — the decision to spend more time cooking and eating healthily had more urgency and purpose. This is key to making change. Once purpose is understood, happiness is an inevitable by-product. "Once the reason is found, however, one becomes happy automatically" (Frankl, 2006).

So, how did I find purpose for cooking? I knew that cooking healthy meals would help heal my husband, benefit my children, help us bond even more as a family and could give me another opportunity to show them and myself love. Sound simple? Even cheesy? Maybe to some. But it gave me a sense of purpose that I needed when I realized the impact, I could make for each of them. Once I gave this clean eating some serious effort, the pay-off and happiness turnaround was incredible.

"Do I really have to do meal planning?"

For this spontaneous gal, planning ahead is a struggle. However, so many nutrition experts will tell you planning is key and I have been burned enough times to know that. I do not thrive when every minute of my day is planned out. That is not what I am suggesting here. Unless you want to and you're the kind of person who does well organizing everything in extreme detail. Know and honour thyself!

For me, slowly over time, my sheer loathing of being in the kitchen became less and less each day. I became more confident in what I was cooking because it was starting to taste good. Unsurprisingly, this helped a lot! Man, let me tell you… some of the stuff I made tasted so bad! The frustration of the wasted effort was not helpful *at all*, but still I persevered. I discovered food blogs, found recipe books I loved, and reached out to friends who ate mostly plant-based and gluten-free. It got easier and easier. I started to plan meals and get strategic with where I shopped for groceries. I organized my kitchen to simplify my life. I continue to do all this, because I am realizing it's an evolution and some weeks are more successful than others. In our family, we opted for healthy vitamin supplements to make sure we all were getting what our bodies needed. It was amazing. When we fed our bodies with healthy, good quality, organic food, we felt so good.

Eating well isn't the be-all-end-all fix to choosing happy, but we can all make the choice to eat a little better. The feel-good return on that effort is powerful. Do we cheat and have potato chips every so often? Absolutely! But in moderation. When we eat the not-great stuff, we feel it, so we choose it only 20% of the time. It drags us down when we don't eat well. And on the journey of choosing happy, we certainly want to limit what doesn't serve us.

No Guilt!

If you do happen to eat something that isn't the greatest for you, *please, please, please* don't jump on the guilt train. Acknowledge your choice and then let it go. Feeling guilty about eating something will only take you further away from your ability to connect with your happy. Guilt does not serve anyone. It keeps you trapped. If you notice the guilt moving in, take action steps to show yourself how you could choose differently next time.

Action time:

Here are a couple of cool ideas that help bring awareness to how food may be impacting your mood.

Food journal

Make the commitment of keeping a food journal for one week. Write down what you ate at each meal and jot down how you feel throughout the day. At the end of the week, review what you ate and how you felt. See if you can notice any patterns. Every nutritionist I've worked with has asked me to do this exercise. I admit it's a bit tedious, but wow! So much valuable information in this!

Invite friends over to bulk-cook healthy meals and snacks

Truth be told, I have not implemented this one as much as I would like! When I do, though, it's a saving grace. I've had friends over to batch-cook. We would double up on the quantities for the recipes we chose, so we both had snacks or meals to take home. We would catch up and have tea together at the same time. It brought in a social aspect to cooking, which is important to me. It also made cooking *way* more fun and was a great way to swap recipes.

Make a meal plan ahead of time

Meal planning must be mentioned again, because it makes life so much easier and saves on the pocket book as well. This isn't as permanent a fixture in our lives as I would like it to be. We still struggle with the commitment to the meal plan. Yet when we do it and batch-cook ahead of time, it frees up a lot of brain space during the week, allowing for more happy choices. We have also during busy overwhelming times paid for a holistic nutritionist to create meal plans for our family. This has honestly been a life saver for our family. The big thing for us was when both my husband and I were in deep with work having the meals thought out for us was HUGE. This helped us stay on track with how we want to eat and took the frustration out of trying to tap into brain power that just wasn't available after an exhausting week.

Think baby steps

Cooking and doing it well was hard for me to build into my routine on a regular basis. I had to take one step at a time, as it easily became overwhelming, the opposite of happy! Each week, I would celebrate when I made a change or tried a new recipe. And each week, it got easier. I learned to ride with the weeks that were tough, because I knew I would continue to chug along and work through my mistakes.

    Choose one improvement every week to focus on. Understand that any step in the direction of healthier eating supports your ability to choose happy.

Resources

Here are a couple of cookbooks and resources for learning how to eat healthily and cook yummy food. These are all tried and tested by me, the non-super-cook. If I can do it, so can you. The difference in how you'll feel will be incredible.

> *The Simplicity Kitchen by Jenn Pike*
> *Oh She Glows by Angela Liddon*
> *The Undiet by Meghan Telpner*
> *Oh My Veggies blog*

CHAPTER 6

Meditation

Over the years, I have taught yoga and happiness workshops, and throughout my own practice, meditation has dramatically shifted in importance. What I find interesting with meditation is that people tend to have a varying degree of receptivity to it. Some people are all for it and others see little value in it. I used to be one of those people who wasn't necessarily resistant to meditation but put it low on my list of priorities. Over time, though, I have come to understand the incredible impact that meditation has for choosing happy. Meditation is now a daily practice for me even if I only have two minutes to dedicate to it. I am committed to integrating it into my life consistently and it is a significant component of my workshops.

Scientific evidence supporting the unbelievable impact of meditation abounds. Just Google 'meditation and happiness' and you will see the number of research articles that pop up supporting the link between the two.

One particularly fascinating study performed by neuroscientists focused on a Tibetan monk named Matthieu Ricard, a 66-year-old geneticist and 'world's happiest man'. Results were profound. In his own words, "Meditating is like lifting weights or exercising for the mind," Ricard told the Daily News. "Anyone can be happy by simply training their brain."

In this study, researchers looked at monks doing over 50,000 rounds of meditation and noted significant changes in brain function. They also observed changes in brain function after three weeks of meditating 20 minutes per day. Ricard states that anyone has the ability to be happy by integrating these meditation habits into their lives.

But just because we know something is good for us doesn't necessarily mean we will do it. As with my own initial response to meditation, I have noticed the same resistance with my yoga practitioners and Choosing Happy workshop attendees even when they understand the great return on investment. Not everyone is fully aware of the powerful impact of meditation and that may be the reason for not embracing a regular practice. It used to have a certain stigma attached to it; it was only for 'those' people (whatever that even means). Fortunately, the label seems to be lifting. Countless articles claim that top executives use regular meditation practice as a success strategy. Given all the positive evidence, I was curious what holds people back from meditation. I decided to ask.

Here's what I found when I surveyed people on what was preventing them from participating in something that can offer so many benefits...

Intimidation

Some found meditation intimidating and were afraid of their own thoughts. Being afraid of connecting with their own thoughts is a powerful indicator that healing is needed prior to being comfortable and landing in their own meditation. The irony is meditation has the ability to provide that healing. (Later in this book, I share healing modalities that helped me get more comfortable in my own skin and led to improving my ability to meditate.)

Time

Another barrier that often came up was time. Telling you how to allocate your precious time is not something I will do. We all have different priorities in our lives. To me, feeling fulfilled and happy is top. When I feel disconnected from my life or my happiness, I'm willing to make the necessary changes and choices.

As I have said before, we all have the gift of choice and sometimes we are presented with choices that we don't necessarily want to make. If happiness is something you want but aren't experiencing and you don't currently incorporate meditation in your life, choosing to meditate instead of doing something else such as watching TV, scrolling on social media or spending time on YouTube may be a choice you have to make. You must execute on the actions that will render you happier if you want to choose happy. Sitting still and being in your own space is extremely beneficial and effective for happiness.

Not having time to meditate is an *excuse*. We can make excuses for anything, including not having time to be happy. To maximize the choice of happiness, you will need to make a commitment to yourself and hold yourself accountable for how you choose to fill your time. Meditation is a *practice*, which means it takes time to figure out and connect with it. When working with time restrictions, step back and observe how often you are watching TV, on social media or simply procrastinating; the solution may mean simply swapping some screen time for some you time.

Many meditators find it beneficial to practice either as soon as they wake up or right before going to bed. The only issue with right before bed is you may fall asleep and sleeping is not the same as meditating. Relaxation is also not the same as meditating. During one of spiritual teacher Marianne Williamson's talks, she explained the difference between relaxation and meditation, relaxation being somewhat similar to sleep and meditation inducing a relaxation response but also creating a shift in brain waves. Meditation requires a certain level of inward focus to have this cerebral impact. Relaxation reduces levels of the stress hormone cortisol but it does not influence brain waves in the same way meditation does.

With that distinction made, let's return to timing. For some, scheduling meditation just like you would schedule a meeting works well. Make it a priority and commit to yourself. If you miss a day, give yourself a break and keep trying. It takes time to create a practice and integrate meditation into your life, but once you do, you will not regret it.

When embracing the happiness groundwork, it can become extremely daunting to introduce all these practices at the same time. Just like cooking and exercise, think one step at a time. Allow whatever you are working on to become fully immersed in your life. Then add in the next bit when you are ready. It is extremely difficult to quiet the brain when we are taking on too many tasks. I have observed this within myself and with so many others who take on new happiness habits with this crazy sense of urgency. This isn't new advice by any stretch, but it is a necessary reminder. Stop and take a deep breath. Or maybe 20! Then begin to consider how you will schedule your meditation practice into your daily life.

Doing it Wrong

Over and over again, I've heard clients worrying that they're not getting it right. Honestly, though, it's difficult to do meditation wrong, unless you're watching TV or something! Then no, that is not meditation. If you're sitting in a quiet space, though, either listening to a guided meditation or simply following your breath as best you can, but maybe getting distracted by your to-do list or a conversation you had in the day... that is *still* a meditation practice. It's a practice where you are working on developing your skill.

As soon as you notice your thoughts beginning to wander away, come back to your breath or listening to the guided meditation. You may have a 'bright shiny objects' moment where it feels like every two seconds your thoughts are taking you on some wild journey. Trust me... you are not alone! In time, with some effort and commitment, you will train and calm your thoughts so that the span of time between getting distracted becomes longer and longer.

Here's a quick tip. Some people need to release energy before they are capable of sitting still for an extended period of time. Going for a walk, playing sports or practicing yoga first can be a great way to get energy out of the body, giving you the ability to focus your mind. It is said that the purpose of the physical practice of yoga is to prepare the mind and body for meditation. Don't be too hard on yourself if you struggle with sitting still, especially if you are what some would call 'an A-type personality'. If this is you, get acquainted with meditation through a moving practice. And if not, yoga may still be a great gateway into meditation.

If you enjoy yoga, turn your entire session into a meditative practice. This can be done by choosing a specific physical sequence, also known as asana, and repeating it over and over on a daily basis so your body gets familiar with the movements. When you no longer need to focus on what pose you do next, shift your focus to your breath and the sensations in your body while you move through your yoga practice.

At the end of this book, you will find a few yoga practices that you can turn into moving meditations. While practicing, turn your focus inward and pay attention to your breath, each practice takes around 20 minutes.

Walking meditations are an extremely beneficial way of meditating. Some find it much easier to reach a calm mental state this way. As mentioned in the previous section, a walk could be a relaxing experience, but not necessarily a meditation, because the mental focus on walking is an essential ingredient of meditating so that a shift in brain waves occurs. In order to make this practice meditative, take a walk, in nature and quietly focus on each inhale and exhale, or repeat an affirmation that is meaningful to you. Even for the seasoned meditation practitioner, a walking meditation can have a powerful impact.

Taking a meditation class from an experienced meditation teacher gives you support and guidance so that you become more comfortable and confident with meditation. There are also great online resources and books at the library that provide wonderful information on how to improve your meditation practice. You could also try a course called Transcendental Meditation, which has powerful testimonials of its incredible results. There are also great apps like Headspace and Calm, that offer many guided meditations.

Finding a Place

I'm a firm believer that you can practice meditation anywhere. I've done it on airplanes, in airports, while waiting for my kids at hockey practice, you name it. To sit with your eyes closed in public and check out so you can check in takes courage, but there have been times where it has served me incredibly well. Having a grasp on how to drop into meditation gives you the ability to practice in public.

That said, creating a space in your home where you can find some peace, quiet and calm is a helpful way to begin and practice. You may have the space to dedicate an entire room or you might be able to create a little corner. Having pictures, flowers or smells that make you feel calm will help you set the tone. If you can paint the space a calm color you like or even have a pillow to sit on in that color, it may help shift your mindset and induce a sense of serenity.

When I was pregnant with my first son, I attended this fantastic pre-natal course where our instructor told us to bring in pictures, music or an object that made us feel relaxed when we looked at it. She taught us that relaxation is a learned and conditioned response. Therefore, prior to going into labour, we were told to practice connecting with this particular item so that it stimulated a relaxation response when we saw it in the midst of labour. My husband and I brought pictures of special memories with us and created a playlist with music that was meaningful to both of us. When I was between contractions, we had these amazing conversations about past memories, and I was able to manage the pain of my labour. I was fortunate enough to be able to deliver both of my children without any drugs or intervention. I realize this is part luck and also part intentional effort. It took practice and preparation to get me to this point of being able to deliver without intervention. That doesn't mean it wasn't difficult and exhausting. It definitely was! Yet it was incredibly worth it. There is no doubt in my mind that my mindfulness practice played a pivotal role in managing the pain and fear that came up in labour. It provided that extra bit of support, drive and focus that I needed. With my first son, I pushed for four hours so it was no joke.

This story is just one example of the impact that training the relaxation response can have. I played my playlist at home in advance, such as when I was in the bath or hanging out with my favourite people, so when I heard the music it made me feel safe. When we create a space where we feel safe and supported, the transition into meditation can be that much simpler.

Feelings of Panic or Overwhelm

Some of my workshop participants have told me that when they try to meditate, they feel panicked or overwhelmed. They say meditation feels like they are reconditioning this anxious response instead of creating a sense of calm. Obviously, this is the exact opposite of what we are hoping to achieve in meditation.

In creating a safe and calm space, it may be helpful to connect first with an object, picture, sound or even specific song to start to train a relaxation response preparing you for your meditation practice. Have the particular item or song around you while taking a bath, reading a book or cooking (if that relaxes you). This way, when you go to begin your meditation, the song or object will help to alleviate any sense of panic, thereby creating a manageable state of mind to move into your meditation.

Next tip: start small. Give yourself the goal to sit for even just two minutes. As your sense of panic diminishes, gradually and compassionately increase the length of time you try to meditate.

Some meditation instructors advise leaning into the fear, even asking yourself what's the worst that will happen while you take time to pause. It can be powerful to sit and experience the panic, working through it, making the fear less and less of a threat over time.

CAUTION: This can be valuable for some and detrimental for others so know thyself.

Keep Trying

Once you decide you want meditation to be a part of your life, remind yourself it's a skill that takes time to develop. In the beginning, you may not see the immediate impact, so it will require a leap of faith to keep going. The length of time it takes to meditate to the level you want is individual. Be patient, kind and compassionate with yourself!

A practitioner in my yoga class has been coming for over three years. Penelope is highly disciplined with her yoga practice and does three classes per week as consistently as possible. However, meditation challenges her in the extreme. She is a busy executive, who many would call an extreme type-A personality. I once heard someone use the phrase 'a triple A personality'. Penelope would likely fall into that category. She loves her yoga practice and often says moving in yoga and doing sports are her meditation. That is a start. In my opinion, she gets full credit as meditation is such a challenge for her.

After all this time of practicing, she still struggles with her meditation practice, as it doesn't look the way she would like. She sits at the end of each yoga class and continues to try meditating. Penelope still finds it intimidating, overwhelming and frustrating at times. However, what matters is she keeps at it every single week. She understands the benefits and persists with the type of meditation that is accessible to her right now, while learning to master what others would consider a more traditional style of meditation.

Key here is that she meditates in some capacity, instead of giving up and dismissing it, which realistically she could. Penelope continues to be open to suggestions and growth in her practice. She is able to sit still for longer periods and can stay more present in her physical practice, which is extremely beneficial and shows progress.

If you are struggling with meditation, you really aren't the only one. Don't take that as a sign you should stop or that it isn't meant for you. How many times have I been taught something and not been able to do it, but then finally got it much later when someone repeated the very same advice? Information resonates differently depending who I learn it from or when I learn it. I am able to assimilate it and integrate it into my life when the teacher or time is right. If you find the meditation groundwork (or any other elements in this book) aren't clicking, simply read the section again until it lands.

As discussed previously, our brains have a limited capacity for information. If you were only able to only focus on one particular aspect of meditation, and found yourself getting distracted, that's normal. The moral of the story is, keep on trying and do not give up. Meditation truly is the magical gift that can bring so much clarity, understanding and focus. As the science and personal experiences of so many can attest, it can truly help foster your ability to choose happy.

Action time:

Grab your calendar and pencil in some dates to hop on the meditation train or go online to set yourself up with a meditation course. Check out a couple of these meditation resources; they are a fantastic place to start and mostly free.

- Search YouTube for any of Louise Hay's meditation videos. They are great!
- Purchase the amazing 21-day meditations by Deepak Chopra and Oprah. These series are that perfect length of time and number of days to create a mental shift.
- A costlier option, the transcendental meditation course has discounted rates for students and options for those struggling financially. Explore their website ca.tm.org.
- There is also the apps Headspace and Calm which are great.

I have also included a few meditations in the appendix. If you prefer guided meditations, record your own voice or the voice of someone you love reading the meditation from the appendix, so you can be guided through it.

This internal connection that meditation can create is valuable in fostering and building a greater degree of happiness. It gives you guidance as to behaviours, actions and beliefs that support or diminish your ability for being happy. When you can make choices through your actions and behave in a way that supports your happiness, you are making a stand and advocating for yourself, saying no to what depletes you and saying yes to what makes you happy.

When you are completely connected to that internal feeling of happiness that meditation creates, you can feel when situations deplete you or nurture you. Sometimes you can't avoid the depleting situations, but you can do something about how you react to them. It is possible to not allow these difficult situations to take over and convince you that your happiness has been 'taken away'. Instead, simply acknowledge the situation for what it is: a challenge, something that goes against your internal truths or values. Then decide what to do about it...

- Perhaps you go to your journal to get your thoughts and feelings out.
- Perhaps you advocate for yourself in order to feel that person inside has been honored.
- Perhaps you call yourself out on your BS, recognizing you are the one creating the depleting situation in the first place.

Later in the book, we dive deeper into this conversation. But before that, know this... beyond the science, your meditation practice can bring clarity and connection to your happiness journey, a greater ability to connect with your personal power and an authentic chance to choose happy.

CHAPTER 7

Random Acts of Kindness

Never underestimate the power of doing something kind for another human. When I am struggling, funky or stuck, random acts of kindness are the best instant pick-me-up. These are highly recommended.

Before I go on, I must reiterate that this work isn't about *dismissing* your feelings of anger or discomfort. It's important to be honest about the way you feel and process your feelings. However, exercise caution around the belief that your life is filled *only* with anger and discomfort. I don't know about you, but I certainly have days when my behavior and mood are nothing short of venomous... sometimes not for good reason either! On those days, I find myself snappy, short and irritable with my children, my family and my friends. On one occasion, my son said to me, "Normally, you are a nice little old lady but today you are more like Godzilla" as he snarled and waved his arms over his head like claws. I'll be honest. Behaving like Godzilla is not how I want to intentionally show up. Yet there are days when life feels crazy heavy and overwhelming; breaking that cycle is tough.

So, what's the solution to funky behaviour? I find it helpful to have friends and family who will call me out when negativity takes over and is frankly unnecessary. However, just because someone tells me I'm behaving like a jerk doesn't mean my mood changes instantly. I am not able to reconnect with my intention of choosing happy 'just like that'.

There are days when choosing happy seems inaccessible. On those days, someone telling me I'm being an ass can just add to the pile. When I feel crap inside, the effort to not be reactive to those around me can be extremely challenging and exhausting, even though they don't deserve an attitude.

The most accessible remedy in this scenario? Random acts of kindness. AKA RAKs!

I love random acts of kindness for multiple reasons. When I am festering in a funk, they truly are *the* most effective solution to raise my spirits. Even just watching a video of *someone else* doing a random act of kindness shifts how I feel in that moment. This is evidence enough of just how powerful they can be on those giving and those receiving. Random acts of kindness create that instant gratification feedback loop of happiness the moment you do one. Your entire perspective changes. A sense of lightness washes over you.

Time to get creative! The easiest go-to RAK I've used is paying for the next person's order at the drive-through. Top tip: drive away as fast as is safe, so they didn't know it was you. One time I had someone stalk me down across four different sets of lights ecstatically honking their horn. I heard the horn at the previous three lights but didn't realize it was directed towards me until the fourth light when I saw this man frantically honking, waving his Tim Horton's cup in the air and mouthing 'thank you' over and over. It created this amazing conversation with my kids, who also thought it was hilarious. In the past, I had never seen the reaction of someone whose order I'd paid for, so this situation was entertaining and gratifying.

I have had people pay in advance for my coffee or meal in the past, so I knew it felt nice. However, I've also been burned with a $20-plus lunch bill before, so now I research random acts of kindness in advance! You don't have to spend money to create value for someone, and you don't want to drain your bank account or create a different stress in your life.

To my great delight, I found an entire website dedicated to random acts of kindness at randomactsofkindness.org. The suggestions are fun and take away the effort of having to think of an idea yourself, which in some instances can act as a barrier to getting started.

Need a little evidence-based research? As always, there is plenty.

Research demonstrates that when someone sets a specific goal to do something for others, the individual who performs the act sees an increase in happiness from a prosocial perspective (Rudd, Aaker and Norton, 2014). And according to the documentary *Happy*, doing acts of kindness or giving back to your community is a proven component for happiness. (By the way, if you haven't seen it, this is an absolute must-watch.) Thus, there's a simple choice you can make to improve your own happiness by doing something kind for others.

The key is to break it down on a more simplistic level. To get that happiness feedback loop happening, think specific. Whether it's smiling at every stranger you make eye contact with, going into a parking lot and putting away someone's grocery cart or picking up litter in the street, when the random act is specific and gets accomplished, happiness is the by-product.

It takes effort and action to do a random act of kindness. Sometimes you may not feel like you have the energy. This is where pushing through may come in. Trust that you will feel better once the action or activity is complete. It's kind of like the 'fake it till you make it' mentality. The cool thing with random acts of kindness is: once you engage in that initial act, the happier, lighter kickback will happen.

The clue is in the name with random acts of kindness... You have to *act*, take action. The hurdle may seem huge at first, but take a leap, do the RAK and watch how you feel.

Action time:

Head over to randomactsofkindness.org and choose three different random acts you are willing to do.

Next, set a deadline for completing these particular RAKs and hold yourself accountable. Writing down your ideas can be exciting; however, it's extremely important to follow through with this one and implement the action, because that is where the true magic begins and how you become happy through these acts.

Finally, after completing your action of choice, take a moment to write down how you felt prior to participating in your RAK and how you feel now you have completed your RAK. Keep these words as reminders for the next time you're struggling with happiness. Know that a random act of kindness could help lift the funky fog.

Bonus tip! Your own experience can serve as a dose of inspiration to get you taking action, so take the time to journal these activities. As we will explore in the next chapter, how journaling feeds another Happiness Groundwork Tool, so it's a double win.

Here are a couple of suggestions to get you started.

RAK Suggestions

Compliment servers at a restaurant on what a good job they're doing.

Leave a note on the receipt to thank them when you pay.

Spend five minutes writing a letter to someone you are grateful for.

Hold the door open for someone.

Donate your hair if it's long enough. (My husband who is bald would not find this one accessible.)

Offer to put away someone else's grocery cart.

It's also fun to get others involved and create a RAK challenge among your friends and family. Kindness spreads and so does happiness.

Just like any groundwork for choosing happy, sometimes you will have to grit your teeth and push through your own resistance or lack of motivation to participate in a random act of kindness. Make sure you do! Then sit back and notice what happens. It is nothing short of amazing.

Dive in deep with this. Be ready to recognize just how much this intentional choice can show you your powerful ability for choosing happy.

CHAPTER 8

Journaling and Gratitude

Whenever I read about the daily habits of the successful and famous, journaling and gratitude always come up. Take Oprah, for example, to name just one. However, I haven't included journaling and gratitude work as happiness groundwork simply because people I admire are doing it, but because once again, the science backs it up (Frein and Ponsler, 2013). From my own experiences and that of clients and workshop participants, I have witnessed incredible shifts.

Journaling and gratitude work go hand in hand. Whenever I write a journal entry, I always start or finish by noting three things I am grateful for. Focusing on just those three things is a great way to start journaling, if you find journaling intimidating or don't know how or what to write.

Once you make the commitment to gratitude journaling, it has the incredible impact of helping shift your perspective. You begin *looking* for things to be grateful for, it allows you to see the beauty that exists in the world and your life in an entirely new light. Seeing your life in a new way shapes your ability to choose happy.

Sharing Gratitude

In my family, we sometimes have a gratitude sharing circle where each member of our family has to share five things, they are grateful for. It doesn't happen perfectly every week, but when we do remember, it's crazy powerful. I first came across the idea in Elizabeth Gilbert's *Eat, Pray, Love*. My kids' goal now is to make Mommy cry happy tears with their gratitude sharing. (Getting me to cry happy tears isn't actually that difficult so they tend to manage this on a regular basis!) Bringing this into our family has created meaningful conversation and helped shift my husband and children's focus as well. At times, my youngest will roll his eyes and not want to participate. However, with a little support and encouragement, he eventually joins the fun. Our gratitude circle also brings up happy memories and gives me more detail and insight into my children's week.

As with random acts of kindness, sending someone a gratitude letter is another way of connecting with how grateful you are. Journaling afterwards about how that experience made you feel can weave together three powerful happiness groundwork practices at the same time.

Introspection

Not only is journaling great for gratitude, but it's also a phenomenal outlet where you can release pent-up emotions and gain clarity and insight on thoughts or situations that may be troubling you. When leading yoga, I often tell students the same piece of advice that has been told to me in class so many times: your greatest wisdom exists inside of you. Same goes for journaling. It peels back the layers and distractions that the external world often creates. When we start to find that deeper connection to ourselves through journaling, solutions to unsolvable problems may arise and clarity on the most challenging of problems can emerge.

When journaling, it can be helpful to ask yourself questions, or you may just want to recount the day's events and how they made you feel. It's completely up to you. Just like you would check in with a family member, friend or co-worker, use your journal to check in with yourself. Your journal can behave as your internal barometer, where you can see if anything feels off or wants to be expressed. Happiness is a unique experience for everyone, so in order to foster your own, it's important to be in tune with your personal needs and have a platform where you can hear your heart's longings.

Having the opportunity to look back and read what you have written about in the past is a cool aspect of journaling. This is a great way to find inspiration or insight into your own healing process, reminders of previous happy events or people who have inspired you, patterns and habits that have worked for you or those that no longer serve you.

Action time:

Choose one or more of the questions below and answer it in your journal. Should you feel inspired to continue writing once you feel the answer is complete, keep going until you have exhausted all your thoughts and feelings or simply said what you want to say.

What really makes me happy?

When am I at my happiest?

When am I at my unhappiest?

How often did I feel unhappy today?

How often did I feel happy today?

What one thing could I choose to do differently that would contribute to my future happiness?

Clarity

When you answer these questions, you have the opportunity to get to know what is working for you and what isn't. These questions are simple guidelines to get acquainted with journaling. However, if none of them speak to you and you feel inspired to go in a different direction, please do. Should you choose to work with these questions, here is where they can be of some value…

In the simplest terms, once we have clarity about what feeds our happiness, we do more of what works and less of what doesn't. Sometimes doing less or more of either isn't that simple, though. Some work may be involved to help shift situations that 'steal' your happy. Such work doesn't always mean getting away from the situation. It can mean sitting in it and healing the issue so that the circumstance no longer has a hold over you or the ability to take away your power, rendering you unhappy.

Adding the support of a trusted therapist, coach or friend can be extremely valuable here. Sometimes the insight of a trusted outsider can give us the clarity we need to move forward and release the hold on us that situations can have. This release allows us to be more aware of where we can implement our ability for choice. Understanding that we need help and what kind can come through that personal connection to our innermost self by way of journaling.

Of course, journaling can then help you refocus and remember that good things happen too. It's so easy to focus on the negative and let that take over. Negativity behaves like a virus, rushing through us without our being aware that it's consuming our choices, our conversations or our perception of reality. When this happens, the light that shines on what makes us happy gets dimmer and dimmer. Journaling is a tool for shining that light again.

So easily we forget... I've had many conversations where people were venting or lamenting; when I ask them to tell me something awesome that happened that day, they stutter and seem lost for words until they refocus their attention. Soon, they remember that indeed something awesome *did* happen that day. Journaling behaves as that stop in the tracks. We intentionally shift our focus. We quit being funky or negative. We realize that, despite all the crap, something great still happened. We simply forgot about it or were too caught up in the BS to pay attention to it.

Some would argue that 'looking on the bright side' is being delusional, which I find interesting. If that event really did happen, why doesn't it deserve the same amount of attention as the not-so-great stuff? That's not being delusional; it's being *more* realistic, in fact, because the good stuff happened too. The news is a perfect example of how we are conditioned to look only at the negative. Car fires, shootings and the stock market are not the only events that happened in any given day. We need to recondition ourselves to open our perspective to both the good and the bad.

"With great power comes great responsibility..." I love this Spiderman saying, because we do all have to take responsibility for our own happiness and recognize where we are investing ourselves. Journaling can give you this amazing insight. Two of our greatest happiness powers are energy and focus. If you are wasting or dispersing these powers, your ability to be aware of your choice will be limited! It's so important to regroup and be responsible for how to allocate your energy and focus.

Invest these powers into your own happiness. Rather than looking back critically or angrily at your journaling and realizing your power has not been allocated in the direction you had hoped, simply make the change. This change may or may not be easy, but just because something is hard doesn't mean it's impossible. Why not journal about your journey along the way?

Action time:

Pick a journal you like.

I have a mild obsession with inspiring journals filled with colours and quotes, so my collection is slightly over the top!

Maybe a simple notepad is good for you. Maybe you prefer a binder. My husband bought a journal but renamed it his 'book of serious things'. It looked like something out of an Indiana Jones movie. The simple decision of choosing a journal he liked made it more accessible to him and that meant he used it.

You don't want your journal to be a source of fear, resentment or aggravation, so choose something that makes you want to go back to it again and again.

Choose a pen you like.

I know some people who use an entire rainbow of Sharpies to journal (that would be me) and others who use the same black ink pen every time.

Choosing writing tools that bring you joy can create an experience. Make it a positive one! The little things do add up. If something so simple as a pen can put a smile on your face, then why not do it?

Timing

Journaling does not have to take a huge amount of time for the gift you will receive in return. You can choose the time of day that makes best sense for you. Be it first thing in the morning, or right before bed, on your lunch break or something else. The important part is you do what suits you. Personally, the lunch break timing I find pretty cool, because bringing a sense of happiness and connection to ourselves right in the middle of the day is powerful and serves as a reminder to be mindful. It is a great place to vent about any experiences that have come up so far in the day. You can release that energy so it doesn't take you down.

Duration

Some people spend significant periods of time journaling, while others may write down just a few point-form notes. Let your journaling experience be personal to you. If five minutes is all you can invest, recognize it is still amazing that you found space to write. Use those five minutes fully. Don't judge your writing if it doesn't look like an epic novel. This is your journal. These are your words, your experiences, your feelings. This is not for others to read. It is for you. And your thoughts and experiences absolutely do matter.

Just start writing, start connecting, see what happens and know you are using your power of choice. And you're choosing happy.

PART TWO: HIGHER INTO HAPPINESS

The Many Sides of Happy

One day, I was having breakfast with a special friend and mentor Tom who also coached me for a few months and where the concept of the 'many sides of happy' came from. As usual, we were musing over the human experience of happiness and discussing the different aspects of what choosing happy means. As you might guess, this topic consumes my life! (I am grateful to have others around me who are okay with that!)

My friend told me the story of someone he knew who had lost his wife, the love of his life, to cancer. Shortly before she died, the wife told her husband that his sad feelings over her death had an expiry date. According to the wife, her husband was allowed to be funky or 'off' for one year; however, when that year was up, it was important for him to move out of that phase and find his happy. Indeed, at that one-year mark, he recognized that it was possible for him to be released from the grips of his loss and that he could now see happiness and all the possibilities for his life in a different light. However, the man also understood how important it had been for him to sit in his process for a while, to be on 'that side' of happiness.

As Tom put it, there are many sides to happiness. I couldn't agree more. Ironically, in the name of happiness, it is most important to be able to experience *all* the emotions that we are capable of feeling as humans. These experiences are not the opposite of happiness. They are simply on another part of the full emotional spectrum.

Let me explain. At my core, I define myself as a happy person; those who know me well would agree. It doesn't mean that I don't get angry or sad. In those moments, I have learned to say I am *feeling* sad or I am *feeling* angry. And I do. I feel it. Happiness is still in abundance, though. Even at times when I feel something other than happiness, I am aware that happiness is around the corner. In due time, I will experience it again.

The bottom line is that it's incredibly important to be authentic with our feelings, instead of always trying to behave or be something we are not. Rejecting ourselves and our feelings is the perfect storm for fostering unhappiness. Inauthenticity or pretence breeds anxiety. Author, speaker and researcher Brené Brown discusses authenticity and vulnerability throughout her books *The Gifts of Imperfection*, *Daring Greatly* and *Rising Strong*. It wasn't until she explained the importance of vulnerability and feeling the effects of it that I realized just how crucial authenticity is for choosing happy. Embracing the idea of vulnerability allows us to navigate the different sides of happiness, understand our own boundaries, humanity, needs and areas of growth, and in turn create our own unique complete picture of happiness.

In Part One, we discussed the foundational daily habits that support your body in feeling good and fostering happiness, where the key to the groundwork tools was choice and implementation. Watching an exercise video or reading a cookbook will give you the education on how to do these things, but you have to take action for the results to come. These intentional activities were the groundwork for choosing happy, but it does not stop there.

In Part Two, we recognize there is more work or other work that needs to be done to find the many sides to happiness and have authentic, sustainable happiness. You can put the groundwork in place and still not become happy. In my own experience, there have been times in my life where I have been busily practicing *all* of these tools but was still not accessing the fullest potential of my happiness.

In the beginning of my choosing happy journey and since as a teacher, there were times I believed these foundations were the complete formula. I thought if all the groundwork was in place, anyone who wanted to be happy was good to go. They had happiness in the bag if they followed through with these steps. Not so.

Now, don't get me wrong. This groundwork stuff is powerful. No question about it. Yet, there comes a time where our 'demons' or past hurts have to be addressed or healed in order to live a truly happy life. It's not possible to choose happy unless we spend time on the 'other side' of it. Undoubtedly, this work is challenging; however, it is so incredibly profound in the journey of choosing happy that it would be remiss not to include it in this book. The remainder of this book is dedicated to the healing tools you need in order to deal with the struggles you have experienced and overcome them to lead a happier life.

REMINDER: All suggestions that follow are not meant to replace the help of a professional therapist or counsellor. If you are struggling with anxiety, depression, any other mental health disorder or suicidal thoughts, get the help of a professional.

Breaking Down the Many Sides of Happy

To create a deeper understanding of the many sides of happy and how this plays out in our choosing happy journey, we will look at three different components.

The first is embracing the importance of our other human emotions and recognizing that, when we have these feelings, it doesn't mean happiness has left our lives. Instead, we are simply on another side of it.

The second is about looking at the many roles we play in life that contribute to who we are and how this intertwines to create our experience of happiness.

And the third component to the many sides of happy is the processing, healing and recovery that allows us to move onto the side of happiness where we want to live. Then it's about choosing to live our lives in that space.

Digging deep and working with the many sides of happy can stir up a lot of emotion, conflict and challenge. I encourage you to revisit this section as many times as you need. Be patient with yourself. Sometimes the discoveries or shifts you seek don't happen as quickly as you may want. This work can be tough but is often incredibly rewarding. Remember to take deep breaths, smile and know you deserve to be happy.

CHAPTER 9

Defining Happy

As we begin to dive deeper into the many sides of happy, it's important to explore what happiness means to you. For a significant time, I operated under the auto-pilot idea that everyone 'just knows' what happiness is. However, after working for years in this realm, I have learned that happiness is a unique experience to every individual.

Sometimes can't we all be slightly ego-centric? I know when something is important and exciting to me, I think it must be important and exciting for everyone else too, right? We all know the answer to that... Of course, everyone has different values and priorities. I get it! Not everyone is interested in yoga or my kids' stories (even though they are awesome), but it shocked me to learn that some people aren't interested in being happy. Far more than that. Some are even appalled by the idea of people being happy. For many, happiness is genuinely not a priority. Others feel it isn't possible for them. And sadly, some people have no reference point of what happiness feels like, so they don't see the purpose of striving for something they have no personal connection to.

So, what is this resistance to happiness? I looked into this question further and reached out to my community to gain some insight. The answers I received were enlightening.

In order to be happy, some said it would require forgiveness that they didn't want or weren't ready to give. Others said it would require change and that the fear of change was a greater influence on their life than the pull of the possibility for happiness. These were interesting in themselves, but one response blew my mind. One respondent shared that they felt too 'inadequate' to have a mainstream ideal of happiness. In other words, inadequate for what happiness is 'supposed to be'.

Inadequacy

This shocking statement stopped me in my tracks, which rarely happens, especially if I've had caffeine! But I couldn't help it. *Inadequate for happiness??* I was puzzled. The Google definition of inadequate is 'lacking the quality or quantity required; insufficient for a purpose; unable to deal with a situation or with life'. *Unable to deal with happiness? Lacking the quality required to be happy? How does someone end up there?* I wondered.

I am curious as to how some people can be presented with the worst of situations yet somehow find it within themselves to feel 'adequate' for life, while others in the same situations feel this sense of inadequacy. Sure, inadequacy is a feeling I am familiar with: not 'adequate' as a mom, not 'good enough' as a wife, falling short as a friend, an inadequate cook, more recently wondering if my writing is up to par. If I really want something, though, even if I feel inadequate, I will go for it anyway. It is super uncomfortable, but the promise of the accomplishment at the end is spectacular. However, that pure feeling of inadequacy can kill ambition entirely in some circumstances.

As I reflected, this idea of inadequacy began to make sense. When we look at all the information available on how we connect with happiness – physical activity, being a part of a community, setting goals that allow us to grow – if we feel inadequate, unable to exercise, undeserving of a community, incapable of following through on a goal, then what would possess us to pursue happiness? Feeling inadequate would be a massive inhibiting factor in our ability to introduce crucial components into our lives that enable us to choose happy.

So what factors contribute to feelings of inadequacy?

First up, fear of failure or not measuring up. Some are afraid of the possibility of failure, some are afraid of change and some are simply afraid of everything. In simple terms, not measuring up is the belief that you just aren't good enough. Not good enough to deserve happiness.

This is more common than you may imagine. I can't begin to tell you the number of people I have come across who punish themselves for a lifetime because they believe they just aren't good enough. They don't know what they aren't good enough for, but this belief is so strong that it translates into not being good enough for happiness.

How do we overcome feeling inadequate, having a fear of change or failure, and this idea of needing to measure up to something before we can be happy?

Integrity

This is where a conversation around integrity and honesty comes into play. Reading a children's book with my kids about Confucius, I appreciated the differentiation between integrity and honesty. Honesty is being truthful with others; integrity is being truthful with yourself. How is this helpful? To get over feeling inadequate about happiness, you have to be truthful with yourself about feeling inadequate *period*. Then reflect on the definition of happiness you have been attempting to reach.

Stop for a moment and be truthful with yourself and your feelings around happiness. Maybe you end up admitting that you just don't know what the hell you're doing at this moment. Own it. Just because you may not know what you're doing doesn't mean you don't deserve happiness at all.

What do you do instead? If you feel like you don't know what you're doing, it's time to start gathering information. Information about yourself and about happiness. (This book is a good start!) Admitting we don't know is the first step in turning any problem (like inadequacy) into a motivator. This first step gets us out of the ruminating phase of just thinking over and over how inadequate we feel.

The next step is you have to *quit* simply accepting whatever is unacceptable in your life. If things are bad, feel wrong or inappropriate, *stop* simply accepting them. Easier said than done, I know, but that doesn't mean impossible. You may not be able to solve the problem immediately, but don't throw your hands up and say, "Oh well, maybe happiness is just not meant for me." No way, hell no, notta! That is *not true*! I am allergic to the word *settle*. Yuck! No settling! Feeling defeated or overwhelmed by inadequacy is normal, but it doesn't get to be the final stop.

You need to decide that choosing happy is possible for you. You can then use the uncomfortable feeling that inadequacy provides, and learn and grow as required to get you out of this trap. If you don't yet feel like the life you're living meets your definition of happy, use that yucky feeling to do something about it. Make some choices.

The key aspect of this statement? Those two little words 'your definition'. Have you ever sat down and defined what happiness means to you? If you haven't, you may be living according to someone else's standards of happy. If this is the case, of course you'll feel inadequate, because you don't even believe in the version of happiness you're trying to attain!

So sit yourself down. You're going to define what happiness means to you!

Happiness is...

According to the Google definition, happiness is...

> *Feeling or showing pleasure or contentment*
>
> *Fortunate and convenient*
>
> *Having a sense of confidence in or satisfaction with a person, agreement or situation.*

Here's a little inspiration for figuring out your definition of happiness. Now it's time for you to dig deeper and find what happiness really means to you.

There is only one rule for this exercise. Your happiness definition has to be non-harming. If your definition of happiness is at the expense of someone else or yourself, that is not true, sustainable happiness. It is a whole lotta something else. Other than that, over to you!

Action time:

A great way to begin to connect with your definition of happiness is to write it out. I love this one, of course, because it is an aspect of journaling, so you are tapping into a choosing happy groundwork tool at the same time.

Find a place where you can have some quiet time. If you're a parent, I understand this can be challenging. Try nap time, after the kids have gone to bed, first thing in the morning, or if it's safe to leave your kids unattended for 10 minutes, escape to the washroom to write. (It doesn't have to be glamorous. You're just looking for no interruptions. Also not always guaranteed, even there!)

Grab a blank piece of paper or your journal and a favorite pen. At the top of the page, write 'Happiness to me is...'

Then just start writing whatever comes to mind. In the beginning, you may feel lost for words or thoughts. This is okay, because you may have to do this exercise a few times to connect with your definition. Writing down what happiness isn't can also help refine your definition.

What's important here is pausing to create that connection with your idea of happiness and holding space for yourself. If you end up sitting for the entire 10 minutes without writing anything, no need to get angry with yourself or take that as a sign that happiness isn't meant for you. This is a perfect insight that you have been striving for happiness but not sure what you're looking for.

If this happens, the next step is allowing yourself to be open to *learning* your definition of happiness. Go into that observational mode on a day-to-day basis. Notice when you feel that spark of happiness. Be open to whether that spark would blossom into your definition of happiness or not.

Alternatively, you may find the 10 minutes goes too quickly and you want to keep writing. If this happens, I say go for it. The more you can connect with and clarify your definition of happiness, the better.

This powerful exercise allows you the potential insight to see any missing links. It creates a sense of clarity of where you *thought* happiness was and then where that isn't true for you. It can bring awareness to where you may be denying yourself happiness by choosing to behave in ways that are the direct opposite of your definition of happiness, even if they are meeting others' definitions of happiness. You may even realize you're already living your definition of happiness, but for whatever reason, the blinders are on, preventing you from seeing your happy life.

If you're not sure what a 'definition of happiness' could even look like, let me give you an example using my own. So here goes:

> *To me, happiness is my ability to operate from a place of love, honesty and integrity, allowing my understanding of myself at that time to show up fully in all my various roles that contribute to my life as a whole. Happiness is holding space for my mistakes and others', permitting a sense of peace, contentment, or even bliss. Happiness is also being connected to my boundaries and values, and having the courage to speak up for them when necessary.*

It is truly up to me if I show up this way, as you can see. I am in control of choosing to operate from a place of integrity, honesty and love towards myself and others. Can I do this 100% of the time? No. Sometimes my integrity is compromised. Sometimes I operate from a place of fear instead of love. Does this mean happiness won't be available again? Nope. It means I grow and learn where I can come back to my definition and choose happy once again.

This definition may seem complicated to some. Semantically, you may say it's not happiness; it's something else. This does not have to be your definition at all. However, when I am choosing happy, this is what I am choosing. This is what I am looking for and working to achieve. This is what guides my daily choices. And when this is happening, I am happy. When I feel I am not accomplishing this, I ask myself where in my different roles in life am I not including myself in the equation or where I may be feeling unhappy.

- Am I going against my sense of integrity and beliefs in my role as a mother?
- Am I being dishonest with my friends, myself, my husband or my career?
- Am I behaving in ways that are diminishing love instead of cultivating it when it comes to my body or my treatment of others?

I also need to ask myself why.

Why am I not bringing my definition of happiness into these roles when it contributes to my experience of being me?

The answers to these questions are infinite. However, often when you peel away the detail in the answers, what seems to be left is *fear*. Fear of being judged, fear of hurting someone else's feelings, fear of rejection, fear of loss... Instead of leaning into our fears to allow ourselves to grow, connect and show up as who we truly are, we conform, we bury, we hide and we avoid whatever we are afraid of facing. When we consistently play the game of avoidance, we end up compromising who we are and trading off this false sense of 'keeping the peace', believing it will create happiness when in fact it does the exact opposite. It may create a sense of peace temporarily, but this model is not sustainable and will eventually create an unhappy you.

Honouring Your Definition of Happy

We need to hold ourselves accountable for living by our own happiness definition. To honor your definition, you may be presented with some awkward decisions sometimes. These choices are not always easy or even obvious. However, when you are powered by the drive of your happiness definition, the choice can be much clearer.

Not always, but it can be as simple as saying yes when you want or need to say yes, and saying no when you want or need to say no. By saying what you mean and meaning what you say, you can indeed create an environment of choosing happy, because you honour the person who exists inside. You may disappoint or incur judgment from another party, but always pleasing others at the sacrifice of yourself is not a sustainable formula for choosing happy.

Maybe sometimes you do say yes when you don't feel like doing something yet you know it's for a good purpose or the greater good. When these situations arise, I know I am operating from a place of love. I am still technically honouring a part of my happiness definition. The key is in recognizing that I made this choice because on some level I still *wanted* to do it, not because someone else told me to do so.

When people define their happiness, I commonly see them realize that happiness was there the entire time, but for whatever reason they weren't able to see it until they connected with their definition. Have you ever heard the statement: "they wouldn't know it was there if it hit them on the head"? We can become so caught up with the pull of daily life that we have no idea happiness is already in our lives. We think something is wrong, when everything is right and we just need to open our eyes.

Tapping into Your Greatest Teacher

I went through a phase in my life where I discussed every decision I was about to make with a friend or family member. Sometimes their advice felt right. Other times I would disagree with their suggestion. However, I completely believed that everyone else knew what was best for me. It was almost like I wasn't to be trusted. Not surprisingly to you I'm sure, one day I realized that if I continued on this path I would find myself extremely unhappy because the one person who did know what was best for me in the truest sense was me. I just had to practice listening, advocating and holding myself accountable for any choices I made that went against my definition.

This can be scary and empowering. The more we can connect with and know ourselves, the greater our chance of understanding our definition of happy.

Understanding gives us the insight and courage to make choices, so experiencing happiness becomes not only a possibility, but a reality.

Defining happy can also help in creating affirmations that we truly believe in, rendering the groundwork element of affirmations that much more successful.

Breathwork and meditation are incredibly helpful for tapping into your internal teacher and extracting what happiness means to you. I attended a mindfulness conference with Dr. Dan Siegel where he explained that the breath is the gateway into our internal state of being. In yoga, the breath (called *prana*) is often referred to as our *essence*. When trying to tap into the internal teacher that we all have, we need to pause, take some deep breaths, turn our focus inward and be willing to connect to ourselves and our intuition.

The number of times I have said to myself, *If I had only listened to my gut...* This is the aspect of yourself you need to access when working on your definition of happy. The information and guidance is in there. You just need to pause, listen... and *feel*. Feeling is the key here. We do a lot of thinking about happiness, but happiness isn't a thought. It's a feeling! You may have seen the quote from the wise and beloved bear Winnie the Pooh, where Piglet asks Pooh, "How do you spell 'love'?" and Pooh replies, "You don't spell love. You feel it." The same applies to happiness.

If the idea of feeling is overwhelming, I get it. Some of us have done a really great job of spending our lives avoiding any kind of feeling, burying them deep down, because we had some pretty horrible experiences. The easiest or most accessible coping mechanism is to go numb.

In the next chapter, we dive further into regaining access to feelings, because it is a key component to the work of choosing happy. You may find it difficult to learn how to listen to your intuition or you may not want to turn inwards. If your brain is busy or chaotic, this is a clue that there may be something deeper to address before you can access your definition of happy.

CHAPTER 10

Roadblocks and the Other Side of Happy

If you don't deal with past thoughts, beliefs, stories, or traumas, they will inform and influence your perspective on the present, including your ability to see where you could choose happy more. Even if you are doing the groundwork, old buried issues will have to be addressed if you want to tap into your fullest choosing happy potential.

Over and over in my career and within myself, I have witnessed how it can feel chaotic, disconnected, messy or inaccessible when we turn inwards. If this is so, there are two issues going on. One, we need more practice. Two, there are old buried wounds or feelings AKA roadblocks.

As I mentioned, when I was sticking to the 'magic formula' of exercise, gratitude, sleep, eating well, journaling, meditating, etc, sometimes I still could not seem to fully choose happy. People reach out to me in the same predicament, saying, "I'm doing all this and still struggling."

Here's the thing. If we hit a wall with happiness, it's a sign that more or other inside work needs to be done. Choosing happy does not mean always feeling happy, remember? Choosing happy means being honest and integral with ourselves and our feelings. In order to have true authentic happiness, sometimes we have to sit on the other side of happiness in grief, anger, anxiety or depression before we can feel a shift.

Depending on the circumstances a person experiences in life, the way they cope with their challenges or tragedies could include burying them down, avoiding them and storing them away because *feeling* them is way too difficult. I recognize how overwhelming sadness or anger can be. There have most definitely been times in my life where dealing with grief was too much to bear. I avoided it, numbed it, pretended I was fine when I wasn't. I've watched hundreds of others do the same. I can remember feeling 'full' on the inside at times; I couldn't possibly tolerate feeling anything more, so shutting off my feelings seemed like the better option.

Sometimes, we convince ourselves that if we bury these feelings down far enough, they will just disappear or go away. The challenge is they don't go away. They remain stored in our subconscious mind and in our physical body. We are all built with only so much space. Eventually, this space fills up and we become so jaded by past experiences that we cannot see the life in front of us. In this scenario, we become completely incapable of seeing the choices available for happiness.

Internal Space for Happiness

Until we feel, release, acknowledge or heal these feelings, we will be filled up with them. This is where the constant strive for more and searching for the next best thing can kick in and convince us that certain behaviours or possessions are the only way to be happy. We will be happy when we… move to the new house or buy the new car or get the new job or sign up for the new membership or get the next promotion or sign the next deal for even more money. I'm sure you recognize some of these quick-fixes. Sure, at times we may find fleeting happiness or glimpses of pleasure while operating from this place of avoidance, but the feeling fades quickly and happiness once again eludes us.

Without healing internally, the ability for choosing happy is not sustainable. Why not? Leaving hurt, struggle or challenges unaddressed while trying to choose happy leaves us susceptible to being triggered because there is no space to process what's happening. This is one reason. Lack of space to process means we operate from a place of reactivity, instead of a place of awareness of choice. The challenge with being reactive is we may say or do things we don't want or mean. Instead of finding happiness, we create complication, distancing ourselves from a deep connection to ourselves and others.

Another reason is lack of presence. Being completely filled with past experiences or future worries means our attention has no space to focus on what is happening right in front of us. As we learned earlier, the brain only has a certain capacity to focus. If it's full of thoughts of the past or the future, physiologically speaking it's impossible to be in the here-and-now. Being able to stay present, we gain access to choice, but we have to be mentally there to actually do it. It takes conditioning or practice to be in the moment. And it's not always easy.

Being present requires us to hold space for the entire human emotional experience and sometimes sit on another side of happiness. Buried-down feelings fill us up with all these avoided emotions and leave no room or time for happiness, because we are too busy avoiding the uncomfortable. We also expend an exceptional amount of energy working to keep these feelings, stories or experiences buried away. Often, when people hear the phrase 'choosing happy', they think it means always focusing on sunshine, rainbows and unicorns; that we should always be happy, regardless of what is going on in our lives. This couldn't be further from the truth, hence 'the many sides of happy'.

Part of the process of authentically choosing happy is honouring that we are human and capable of feeling many different emotions. This is important because this how we learn and grow. This learning and growth is what I mean by the 'many sides'. As so many of my workshop participants report, we are able to understand and appreciate happiness when we have been on the other side of it. These clients understood what the grips of anger felt like. They knew the heaviness of sadness and despair. Similar to the concept that we can't understand the light without the dark. Does this mean we can't understand happiness without being sad? Not necessarily. But through a diversity of experiences and emotions, we will be better informed and capable. Choosing Happy workshop students have explained that experiencing and processing their buried emotions *and* giving themselves the permission to move past these stories led them to connect even more with the beauty and bliss life has to offer.

To move past the stories and hurt though, they first needed to *see* the stories and hurt, process them and heal them. This takes time and tends to happen in layers. Over time, this work allowed them to embrace happiness on a much deeper level.

If we are full, we need awareness and then we must create space inside. Sometimes that means sitting on the 'other side' before coming back onto the side where happiness resides.

Buried Feelings Blur the Choice

Nine months after my father passed away, I received the unthinkable news that I had cancer. At the time of my diagnosis, I had two very young children at home and an incredibly hard-working husband who all needed me in their lives. When confronted with the terrifying scenario, my response was to do everything possible to influence a positive outcome. I went on a clean eating diet. Exercise became an even bigger priority. I saw healers who helped me deal with my past hurt. I held onto as much positivity as I could. The more I healed the past stored-up hurts, the more positivity I could connect with.

Don't get me wrong. I had moments where the fear of my children losing their mother pulled me into a dark hole. I was sad. I was angry. I was confused. Yet I rarely let it show. I held on tightly, keeping my spirits up. I went into surgery with the most amazing support from friends and family, who pulled together and flew out to stay with us during and after my stay in the hospital.

Then at 9:30pm, 10 days after my surgery, I received a phone call from my surgeon. He informed me that they'd found no traces of cancer anywhere else, that all my tests had come back clear, that I wouldn't need chemo or radiation. It was the best possible outcome I could have imagined. I'd followed my choosing happy formula down to a tee, with incredible care and grace on my side.

I felt great. I felt relieved. It was over! Being released from the grips of cancer, which controls some people's lives, creates a serious sense of gratitude. Needless to say, I was in a deeply happy and thankful place.

A year later, I felt drawn to giving back to the cancer community. I realized how lucky I was and that so many others do not experience that same blessing. So I decided to apply to volunteer at a cancer center where people who have been diagnosed or are supporting someone who has cancer can walk in and receive help. I applied to become a peer counsellor, meaning I would listen to people who had just been diagnosed with cancer and hold space for them. It was a full-on role.

In order to become a volunteer, you first have to spend a day with a psycho-therapist to ensure you are mentally prepared. There were 15 people in the room and the introductory activity was going around sharing how cancer had affected your life. I was one of the last people to share my story. By the time it was my turn, I was a sobbing mess and two complete strangers reached out to hold my hands while I tried to retell my experiences. Then we went around the room again and had to share what was happy about our lives today. I exclaimed that I was happy, had a beautiful life and felt grateful, despite my previous response. Later in the day, we had to role play different counseling scenarios. I found it all incredibly tough.

Finally, I asked the psychotherapist if there was a rule about crying with clients. She informed me that we shouldn't be crying more than the person we were working with. At this point, I knew I was in over my head. I was not at a point in my own healing to be able to help others. When I came to this realization, I was devastated. It was time to dig deep and feel some pretty intense feelings that – subconsciously – I had been hoping would just disappear. The fact was the hurt hadn't gone away. I became incredibly aware of past pain that still impacted my life, even though it was in the past. All this time, I thought I'd handled my own experiences with cancer really well, but I was yet to come to terms with my own diagnosis, and my mom and my dad dying from cancer.

In reality, I had done a great job of filling up my time with other distractions. I had convinced myself I was totally cool with all of it. I quickly learned I hadn't processed any of it at all. To be perfectly honest, I was hurting bad. Without being consciously aware of it, I had strategically avoided the process of feeling the anger, disappointment, frustration, fear, resentment, sadness, and many more emotions besides that can come along with being diagnosed with cancer and with losing family members to this disease.

Coming home from my volunteer day, I informed my husband that I felt like I'd been hit by a truck. I was so overwhelmed that even putting one foot in front of the other to make it to the couch felt excruciating. I experienced a flood of the most intense emotion I had ever felt. It took over my being like I was possessed. I went into an intense mood for about three days where I could barely function. Simply uttering 'hello' to my children took the most incredible effort.

In those three days, I surrendered. I sat in all the emotion that had been brewing from my past experiences with cancer. I shifted from devastated with sadness to raging with sheer anger at how unfair this disease was. I cried, I wrote, I slept, I crawled to the bathroom. The whole of my being shattered to the core.

Then on the third day, my husband simply asked with a kind smile, "How are you today?" For whatever reason, it sounded different today. I felt like I was re-reading a book for the 15th time and seeing a message I'd missed the first 14 times. In that moment, it was like someone saying to me: "I know how much all of that hurt, but can you see what is in front of you now?" I experienced a mild sense of peace, then knew I had a decision to make. *Do I continue to dwell in my sadness, anger and frustration or am I ready to be present, to experience life and to receive this beauty that I know is in front of me?* That same beautiful life I had talked about a few days prior with so many strangers…

Allowing Yourself to Process

I knew I had to choose to connect with happiness again with as much conviction as when my father had just come through his heart attack. I had convinced myself somewhere along the way that I had chosen happy once and was good to go. I thought that choice would last forever. Realistically, choosing happy is an ongoing process throughout our life journey. We will constantly be confronted with challenges in life. How we choose to move forward from these challenges is up to us. Amazingly, by letting myself work through the sadness, anger and frustration that I had buried long ago, I was even more capable of seeing all that made me happy. I could truly feel happy again. I freed up the space in my heart and mind that anger over my cancer diagnosis had taken up. By allowing myself to cry about it, by being unbelievably pissed off over the moments I had missed with my children, the worry it caused my husband and family, the physical pain and exhaustion of surgery, by feeling all these 'difficult' feelings, I was able to truly let them go and make space for happy.

I had made a critical error in my previous understanding of choosing happy. Pretending everything is fine is not a strategy for true sustainable happiness. Happiness is not harvested by always putting on a brave face. It's experiencing the *big feelings* that makes us brave. It's experiencing a wealth of emotions on another side of happiness that makes us grateful. The crucial part is we don't have to live there. I allowed myself to lean in to the fear of feeling the hurt or the anger that came along with some of my life's experiences. I knew it would be intense. I was so afraid that if I went down the road of feeling, I would never return to any state of happy ever again. Let's face it. It *was* intense. There was a lot of hurt. This time I had developed tools to help me feel again; those same tools also brought me back from feeling the 'other side' of happy to feeling real happiness again. I needed to do some processing. By holding space for myself to heal, I realized happy was still there waiting for me. I was back where I wanted to be.

What happened next blew my mind. After processing all those feelings, happiness was there in an even bigger and more authentic way than I knew was possible. I just had to be ready and willing to see it.

There is no question that going through this phase of processing is exceptionally hard work. This is often where we want to self-medicate, whether with drink, drugs, food, excessive spending, gambling, the list could go on. We do this to ease the discomfort that surfaces along with our feelings. However, self-medication is a short-term fix that can create a long-term problem. This is where choosing happy can require an exceptional amount of courage as well as support.

REMINDER: These feelings are tough, intense and exhausting. Seeing a therapist can benefit your journey. If you feel you need the help of a professional coach, psychologist or your doctor, don't hesitate to reach out for that help.

Those who suffer with mental health issues may need the support of pharmaceuticals as prescribed by a doctor. Don't take that as a sign that you can't still work on choosing happy. However, please remember that this book does not replace the individualized support of a qualified professional.

In his book *Flourish*, Martin Seligman describes the possibility of people flourishing with mental health issues or languishing but being considered mentally healthy.

A friend who is a child psychiatrist describes the support that medication provides like this, "The medication simply acts as the armour to help the individual feel a little more prepared for their internal battle. However, they still need to do all of the other work to help support themselves in coping with their particular challenges and also to give themselves the opportunity to thrive."

Even if you are supported by medication, it is important to hold yourself accountable for the choices you are able to make to help create your happiest life.

Working with the happiness groundwork tools can create space, but there are times we have to go beyond these foundations and do a little cleaning out and letting go. I have heard people say, "I don't have the time to be happy." Not 'having time' is a code word for needing to do some inside work. Sit down and have one serious conversation with yourself about where your priorities lie. Choosing happy isn't selfish and doesn't take an exceptional amount of time. It takes mere moments. It is a simple in-the-moment choice. Realistically, when you then acknowledge that you are willing to make happiness a priority, the clearing out work gives you at least a little bit of space to begin.

When working through the many sides of happy, there can be times where it is far from light, fun and exciting, which is the usual way many people would describe happiness. Stay connected to the groundwork while doing this inner work, because it serves as a support to help cope with the sometimes intense experiences that come along with being on the other side of happy. An angry run or miserable workout session can be incredibly therapeutic!

How to Hold Space for Your True Feelings

As a young child living with my dad, I would get into arguments with my stepmother sometimes. I would end up in my room crying and the emotion would spill out. Inevitably, my father would come downstairs to have a chat and his advice would always end in "just keep the peace, Mieka." Translation: don't say anything to cause an argument. While this approach kept the peace in the sense of a quieter household (and my stepmother and me fighting less!), it was most certainly not creating peace inside my little being.

Let's face it. Expressing feelings is not always accepted or reinforced in our society depending on where we grow up. However, we have to learn to speak up and honour our emotions even if it creates a 'disturbance in the force' as they say in Star Wars. Now, this doesn't mean going around and giving every single person a piece of your mind. That can come from a vengeful, nasty place. It can also rebound on you to create an unhappier experience. But there are ways to create space to feel emotion.

When you feel sad, give yourself the permission to cry or be gloomy. If you are angry, give yourself the permission to punch a pillow or yell into it. If you need to create boundaries, create the friggin' boundaries. If you need a day to retreat or reflect, practice allowing without any expectation that you need to be different. You do not make this emotional state your new permanent home. Choosing happy is also about what you are going to do next.

You have a certain amount of space inside, before you get full and can no longer focus on life, your job, your family or your happiness. This is why healing from your experiences is so incredibly important.

Interestingly, the experience of being 'full' or hitting a roadblock can show up in many different forms. It can look like stress, lack of sleep, poor concentration, reckless behaviour, disease or illness, anxiety, depression and so on. As much as many of us don't want to admit it, emotion always overrides logic. When we are caught up in the moment, our emotions can make us feel justified for just about any action. These same emotions, especially when bottled up or buried down, can keep us convinced that happiness and joy have disappeared forever. This is a dangerous place to exist as it can create careless and sometimes reckless behaviour, because we think, *I can't be happy anyway so what does it matter what I choose to do?*

Reaching out for help may well be necessary. Don't assume or expect you have to process this all on your own, especially if you are full, not coping, or tending towards recklessness or ill-health. The right support is an invaluable tool.

Many of us have experienced the consequences of our emotional reckless behavior and know that these aren't the type of consequences that tend to elicit happy experiences. Do we all make mistakes? Absolutely. Will we continue to make mistakes? Thankfully, yes. Mistakes are how we learn and feeling guilty is pointless. However, if we continue down the road of reckless behavior once we've become aware of the mistake, then it's no longer a mistake; it's a choice. Such a choice can be extremely harmful to ourselves and others, which is not a definition of happy. This behavior will keep you disconnected. It will take us further and further away from creating the space to find the truest form of ourselves inside. When we have more internal space, the ability to pause, see the emotion before we react and make a choice instead is so much easier.

Everyone's journey is different. However, if you find there are challenging moments — like, excruciatingly hard — know you are not alone. There is no single 'perfect formula' for everyone. To find what works for you to enable you to choose happy, know that you can learn a lot by understanding and feeling the different aspects of who you are.

Over the next few chapters, I will give you tools for healing, processing, letting go and clearing out any emotional roadblocks you come across.

CHAPTER 11

Clearing Out the Roadblocks

To have true sustainable happiness, once we are emotionally ready and strong, it is important to process or heal past challenges from particular times in our lives. This is a hard when we are in a place that feels good; there's a part of us that crosses our fingers and hopes that situations we encountered in the past will just disappear and not affect us anymore. Yet, processing deep-rooted hurt and difficult emotion is the difference between fleeting and sustainable happiness. It can also be the difference between understanding that happiness comes from within and not outside of us. Regardless, eventually, processing the various feelings or emotions that require us to sit on the other side of happiness is incredibly important.

Survival Mode

There are times when we get slammed with a super harsh experience and need to compartmentalize our experiences or feelings as a survival mechanism. Just to help us to keep going.

Before we jump into the whole experience of processing or working on healing past pain, there can be a gap in time where we just put one foot in front of the other, because we have experienced something incredibly challenging or even traumatic. Maybe we are hibernating because the feelings are so big and overwhelming that we need to *just be*.

Looking back at my own grief and trauma, the ability to process in real time wasn't possible. There were times when the idea of eating breakfast felt like the most challenging task imaginable; let alone facing the overwhelming grief of losing a loved one so that I could reconnect with my sense of happiness. There are times when life can be a lot. In that moment, going down the road of processing feelings just isn't possible.

When we think about the path of grieving, most of us understand there are stages that we need to move through before we are able to truly accept, heal and move on with our lives. Even then, it can creep back in years later and derail us. In the beginning phases of the aftermath of an overwhelming experience, it tends to feel like survival mode. Figuring out how to make it through the day or even getting out of bed can be incredibly difficult. When we are in survival mode, we simply surrender and do our best, allowing the opportunity to regenerate some of the energy that has been depleted.

Choosing happy requires an exceptional amount of energy. Although it may not feel like it at the time, we are indeed honouring choosing happy by allow ourselves to simply be. Survival mode is one of those times. Celebrating and acknowledging yourself for completing the simplest of tasks such as brushing your teeth or eating a meal is valuable when you're going through this. The initial shock of trauma or grief can be excruciating. It can stop us dead in our tracks. That means any movement from there counts as progress. In survival mode, it is powerful to acknowledge the baby steps and find anything to connect us to a sense of gratitude or feeling alive. This is extremely important because it provides that element of hope; even if it's only the smallest glimpse or tiniest breath, hope is a reminder or brief awareness that happiness and joy are waiting, even if life is incredibly overwhelming at the moment.

Survival mode is where we need to give ourselves permission to receive any help offered that we deem helpful. There are circumstances where the help available isn't necessarily what we need. It's okay to say no too.

Healing or beginning to reconnect with happiness and joy comes down to being ready. There isn't a magic timeline. When the energy shifts and there is space, we start to reconnect with our ability to choose. In that moment, we begin to hold ourselves accountable for choosing to move forward and ultimately choosing happy.

Action time:

If you find yourself in survival mode having recently experienced a traumatic experience, the very first step is to look at who you could reach out to. It may be a trusted friend, family member, local community leader, your family doctor, a therapist or a church. If help is being offered – the type you want – take it. Allow people to give you that hug, make you that meal, bring that coffee or clean your bathroom.

People like to help. All too often, we take the perspective that we are being an inconvenience. However, when someone loves you, they want to help. Simply letting them in can be an underestimated step in healing.

When I was recovering from my second surgery after my cancer diagnosis, I was blessed with a village of helpers. Was it difficult to have others cooking the meals, lifting up my kids, even getting my groceries? At times, yes. But when I surrendered to it, after a while, having this help allowed my recovery to be that much more successful. And that's what I needed. Life can become difficult. Asking for and receiving help can be a ray of hope that you have the strength to get through.

Understand that asking for help when it's needed is an aspect of choosing happy. One of my favorite happiness authors Robert Holden says, "If you are alive, you need help." I love this notion, because sometimes we believe we are above help or think asking for help makes us weak, whereas really getting stuck in these thoughts can take us in the opposite direction from happy. Cultivating community and connection is a foundation of happiness that can happen when receiving help and people do want to help. Not necessarily everyone, but there are a lot of people who want to help. Letting them, can feed their happiness foundation too through a sense to community connection and helping others.

Extremely traumatic situations that can put us into this survival mode tend to be but not limited to: the loss of a family member, friend or job, dealing with abuse, a break-up/divorce, a disease diagnosis or addiction recovery. Whether it's in your own community or even online, there are so many different support groups out there available to help when we are in this space of barely getting by. These people are experts in holding space at this time.

When we are in this survival mode, it is also helpful to have a quote or two, a favourite smell, plant or photo to serve as a reminder that happiness is around the corner when you are ready to see it again. It may not resonate straight away, but at some point, you will leave survival mode and find the strength to lay the foundation to thrive once more.

Action time:

You may find yourself wanting to push along at work even harder, grind it out and get lost in your day-to-day business so you can avoid the pain of whatever is happening in your life. Give yourself permission to do what you need to do to make it through the day.

Give yourself the permission to cry, punch a pillow, scream, sit silent and stare out the window or into space. Avoid drugs, alcohol, gambling, excessive spending, excessive eating or working until you're burnt out, as these will perpetuate the problem and possibly create another one, moving you that much further away from your potential to reconnect with happiness.

There comes a moment in our experiences when we tend to exit survival mode and start to 'function' again. We re-find our feet and can seem to move on with our lives. It can appear from the outside that the person in question is moving forward. Indeed, this may be true. However, 'moving forward' may come from a place of avoidance and learning to bury the trauma down, instead of genuinely getting on with life from a place of authentic healing. If this pattern continues through every challenging experience we face, eventually we exhaust our internal resources and our emotional health begins to give out. Often, the first resource to disappear is our happiness.

Making the Space

Most of us know what it feels like to be full, done, extremely overwhelmed, at our wits' end. We have no room left for anything, sometimes not even the sound of a loved one's voice. Or we wake up one day and realize we don't recognize or like this person we are becoming. Sometimes we feel this way simply because we *are* exhausted and just need to get through the week. Then there are the times when it's more than just our busy schedule putting us over the top. It's the strategically buried stuff from the past that may have been too much to face or that we didn't have the tools to deal with when it was happening.

When we recognize ourselves in this particular space and should choosing happy be a priority, we become aware of a need to create space emotionally, mentally, spiritually and even physically. In order to do this, we must process those feelings. I will say this again: when moving through a phase of processing, healing or recovery, the support of a professional or trusted loved one is crucial and powerful.

When we decide to process challenging experiences or emotions to connect deeper with choosing happy, we should operate from a place of honesty and integrity about what we're feeling and why. This may take a couple of attempts. Depending on how long ago the difficult experience happened or how many times we have strategically avoided it; there may be a few layers we have to peel away first before we are able to access the true source of what's 'filling us up'. This can sound a little discouraging; however, each layer peeled back is a potent step in the right direction and shouldn't be trivialized.

Action time:

When creating internal space, there are so many tools available to help with processing difficult emotions and experiences. This is just one of thousands of valuable tools.

Find a space by yourself where you can spend at least 30 minutes on this exercise.

To help process and clear out some of these toxic emotions and feelings, it can be incredibly helpful to sit down and write a letter. Getting your thoughts and feelings out on paper helps you gain clarity with what you need to process. The letter may be to a family member, a friend or maybe even yourself.

In this letter, talk about what emotion or experience you've had that you feel is taking up space and getting in the way of choosing happy. Maybe you're feeling angry, frustrated or jealous about a particular situation or something someone said and you can't seem to shake it. Then you write and write to get out all your opinions, your anger, your sadness or your disappointment regarding this particular thing. Maybe you're feeling a certain way but don't even know why. Then start with writing about the feeling, how long you've been feeling that way, why you think it might be clouding your ability for choosing happy. Let yourself experience and feel all the emotions that surface while you're writing this letter.

Cry, yell, punch a pillow, maybe laugh hysterically. Authentically feel. Whatever is taking up precious space and not serving you or your choosing happy journey, release it.

Once you have written all you need to write, take a moment to step back and simply be still. Maybe you will re-read your letter or perhaps you will just breathe. Take some time to reflect with your letter, asking yourself if what you wrote feels true or right for you.

Sometimes we write things down that we've held onto so tightly and deeply for years and then we look at that feeling and say to ourselves, *That's actually not true for me anymore.*

It's okay to change your mind or grow out of certain beliefs and truths you once held dear. Feeling bound to 'beliefs' that no longer hold true can convince you that you don't have any choices. Taking time to let go of the values that don't work for you today — certain 'supposed tos' or 'shoulds' — creates space. Here, you connect with beliefs and ideas that match the person you are today. This opens your eyes to your ability to choose happy.

Reflect on anything you *do* deeply believe in that had been forgotten. Not living according to a powerful intrinsic value can also convince you there is no opportunity for choice, making you feel inauthentic. Trying or pretending to be someone you're not is exhausting. A jaded perspective will *always* limit your ability to choose happy. Connecting to what feels right and makes sense will open space where you were once internally conflicted.

When you've sat with your letter long enough, it's time to physically let go of it and all that you poured into it. Physically releasing all the emotions, thoughts and feelings you invested into a past circumstance or person — and that you have committed to paper — behaves as a metaphor for letting it go. It no longer has to be held inside of you. It is now on the outside, on this piece of paper. Take the letter and burn it or rip it up into tiny pieces.

Next, take a moment to affirm that you are releasing all this past hurt by saying, "I am letting go."

Remember, this letter isn't meant for anyone else but you. It's a place for you to get honest with yourself and your feelings without judgment or urge to please others.

Take a deep breath and embrace the new space you have created in your being.

Sometimes, this is the moment that we want to refill that space quickly... with french fries or wine. Instead, nourish your body with something healthy and nutritious, maybe take an Epsom salt bath or a long shower, and become familiar with how different you may feel by not having this burden on your shoulders any longer.

Getting Familiar with Your New Space

For some, this new space can feel scary, not because it's unhappy, but simply because it's unfamiliar. To continue creating sustainable happiness or a solid platform for choosing happy, we might try detaching from what seems familiar. Familiar doesn't always mean good or happy. Familiar just means we know it. It's possible to be familiar with anger, grief, chaos or stress. Constantly identifying with and feeding these will not render us happy, even if they are comfortable. Staying connected to the familiarity of these feelings can create the opposite: patterns of sabotage. If we are so attached to the familiarity of stress and the comfort that familiarity brings, we end up choosing stress and crushing happy.

Depending on how long we have been disconnected from our happiness or if we have never truly felt happy, then choosing happy may be uncomfortable for a significant time, simply because of how new and unfamiliar it feels. You can repeat this creating space activity as many times as you need. Think of it as a purging. Release all those thoughts and feelings from your mind and your heart so you no longer have to bear the burden of them. Some people make it their job to bear these burdens, stories and pain. Perhaps you believe having that role makes you happy or gives you a purpose. It is okay to change your role. We all deserve to feel love, peace and happiness. I also believe we all need a reminder of this. Make sure you cycle back and check in with your happiness groundwork. When you're struggling with sabotage and getting used to making space inside, this affirmation can also be helpful: "I am safe, I am strong, I embrace the new space I have created."

Stay accountable for your attention and your thoughts so that you don't fill that space right back up again with more stress, tension or anxiety. That space has been created so that you can choose happy.

Using the Body to Create Space

More and more understanding points to memories not only being stored in the brain, but also in the body. Massage therapists, body workers and yoga instructors have recounted stories of profound emotional release or a surge in memories surfacing when working with clients and stretching or moving them in a particular way. Personally, I have experienced this both as a subject and a teacher.

According to an article published in the Journal of Bodywork and Movement Therapies, there is evidence to suggest that after we experience an emotional trauma, collagen structure in fascia can be altered into a hexagonal shape "referred as emotional scar" (Heine, 1990). Wikipedia does a good job defining fascia... Fascia is a band or sheet of connective tissue, primarily collagen, beneath the skin that attaches, stabilizes, encloses, and separates muscles and other internal organs.

Furthermore, we feel better when we release tension held in muscle or fascia through yoga or bodywork. I have heard countless stories of yoga students moving through a practice and finding themselves emotional, but unsure why, or experiencing specific flashbacks. One theory behind this is the shift in the emotional scar of the fascia tissue once it has been stretched or released. This provides a massive relief in both physical and emotional tension; we experience feeling better physically and emotionally. And when we feel better in our physical bodies, it's amazing how much easier it is to choose happy. Conversely, we create a negative mental feedback loop when we hold tension in our muscles and joints, which influences a negative perspective. Therefore, feeling tension or discomfort in the body can convince us that happy choices are too difficult or even impossible, whereas releasing the body's tension by getting into the fascial tissue where 'emotional scars' exist creates more physical space.

Action time:

Once the letter-writing activity is complete, some sort of physical activity (preferably something relaxing, beginning with the mindful intention of letting go) will facilitate the release of the physical tension created from whatever was revealed in the letter. You can foster physical release or removal of tension in the body by taking a yoga class or getting a massage. You could also learn fascial release techniques. Just make sure you work with a qualified professional.

Begin with the affirmation "I am letting go." You could also say "f**k this s**t, I am letting go." Whichever version works for you!

Then mindfully practice letting go of the tension in your body that may be associated with the stories, beliefs or feelings you once held. This action reinforces your healing process and creates space for choosing happy. You don't have to know what you are trying to release from the body.

Alternatively, it can be beneficial to use the affirmation "I am letting go" while moving through a yoga practice or having a massage.

Simply set the platform for releasing those stories, buried emotions and trauma from your physical being and creating space for your happiness.

CHAPTER 12

Mind-Body-Spirit

I have to be honest I hate the term 'woowoo'. I don't even know what it means, but I've heard it used so often when people are referring to dealing with feelings and some approaches used to do this. In my view, I would be doing the entire choosing happy process a total disservice if I didn't include some of the powerful profound healing practices from yoga that tap into feelings and help in creating space, shifting focus and letting go of past hurts. Though this may sound 'woowoo' to some, my most impactful healing came from diving into techniques that this one-time-science-minded gal would have found a little kooky.

Make Room for a Little Woowoo

In order to fully embrace choosing happy, understand we are a mind, a body and a spirit. Don't let the 'mind-body-spirit' term count you out. Mind, body and spirit are all elements of who we are. You may find it tricky to see yourself this way, as a mind, body and spirit. I found it hard to access the idea too and struggled to put it in another way that was relatable until I began my Master's degree.

The first course I took in my counselling and psychology Master's was called 'a bio-psycho-social approach'. From a counselling perspective, it's understood that people's behaviors are influenced by biological, psychological and social elements. Biology: genetics, diet, exercise, pharmaceuticals, etc. Psychology: learning, memory, thinking, stress management, self-esteem, coping skills, etc.

Social: school, family, interpersonal relationships, trauma, spirituality, etc. This perspective acknowledges the intertwining influences that all impact the human experience.

In terms of choosing happy, I recognize that there are multiple components informing our ability to choose. I use the words 'mind, body and spirit', but I know the word 'spirit' doesn't resonate for everyone, so if *biopsychosocial* is a more relatable lens for you, then use that. Let's take a moment to define what I mean by 'spirit' a little further.

Defining Spirit

In really simple terms, my definition of *spirit* means being connected to something that is greater than us. Spirit can be such a complex and subjective definition as well as experience.

When I speak of spirituality in this book, I have a few reference points. One of them is from the book *Spirituality for Dummies*. (I'm not kidding!) Spirituality relates more to your personal search to finding greater meaning and purpose in your existence. Some elements of spirituality include the following:

> *Looking beyond outer appearances to the deeper significance and soul of everything*
>
> *Love and respect for yourself*
>
> *Love and respect for everybody.*

Should your own definition of spirit look different or include elements other than what I have outlined here, allow your understanding of spirit to come through, yet always from a place of love and never harm towards yourself or others. Whether you want to call it the Universe, nature, God, Goddess, it is totally up to you.

One of the most influential people in my life is an activist, international yoga teacher and all-around incredible woman by the name of Seane Corn. She has the most brilliant way of describing spirituality or God for those who may not have a strong sense or any sense of spirit at all. She says, "For me, God is just that which is within that is truth and love. As far as I'm concerned, you could be an atheist on this path and still have a very strong spiritual practice if you practice truth and love."

Healing from those times where we have felt betrayed by truth and love or behaved in a way that betrayed our own truth and love is powerful for creating space to choose happy. When we are connected to our sense of truth and love, we are connected to something that is greater than us: spirit.

The Mind-Body-Spirit Interconnection with Choosing Happy

If something is affecting us mentally or spiritually, it will impact the body. If something is affecting us physiologically, it will also affect us mentally and spiritually. All these aspects of us are communicating to each other and influencing one another. I emphasize this because our ability to choose happy is influenced by everything that is going on physically, mentally and spiritually.

Our thoughts can create a physical experience. In turn, a feeling in our body can create certain thoughts. If the feelings in the body continue, the thoughts can snowball, creating this constant feedback loop of zero control and no connection to choice. What's more, this impacts us spiritually or subconsciously. Tied into this feedback system can be beliefs that we deserve to feel awful because we did something wrong at some point in our lives and deserve to be punished. Hence, we sit in this chaotic mess of an experience, trying to numb it, avoid it or maybe even destroy it. When this is happening in our being, there isn't a lot of room for anything else, including truth, love and happiness towards ourselves and our loved ones. Being caught up in this spiral can make us reactive and resentful in our relationships. It could be with our partners, children or co-workers, anyone really. In turn, instead of treating others with love and compassion, we become venomous and angry, spewing whatever happens to fall out of our mouth. Then we look around for outside negativity to justify why we feel the way we do, instead of stopping to take a really good look inside.

When we understand the connection of the mind, body and spirit, we can see the impact that certain life events have on choosing happy. This is where sometimes just trying to change our thoughts to 'choosing happy' doesn't always work. We may need to release the energy or the experience from our physical body and also embrace healing from a loving, deeper meaning or spiritual perspective.

Needless to say, this all means the mind, body and spirit do not operate as separate entities. They are constantly influencing one another. So, when we are processing a physical, emotional or spiritual trauma, it's important to hold the space to release that trauma from all locations. This will create greater potential for choosing happy.

We've discussed healing and processing tools for the mind and body, but how do we heal and process the spiritual aspect, especially if we are atheist or agnostic? One great place to start is with an ancient system used in yoga philosophy based on energy, because we can all feel energetic and at full energy capacity or depleted and deficient of energy. The ancient energy system I'm talking about here is the chakra system.

I was briefly introduced to chakras when I took my yoga teacher training, but I didn't immerse myself in it until I took a weekend-long chakra workshop with Seane Corn two years after my recovery from cancer. I was excited as I thought I was going to learn some cool yoga sequences, which in fairness I did, but I didn't realize it would stir up all the deep-rooted crap that I had buried deep so many years ago. I received yet another chance to 'let go'.

This exposure to the chakra system gave me a glimpse at the insane possibilities for choosing happy that exist within our reach. To say I cried a lot would be an understatement. To say I walked away feeling empowered would be an even bigger understatement! I gained a sense of total clarity, awareness, peace and freedom that I had never been in touch with before.

The Chakra System

The chakra system has specific points in the body where energy gathers and creates a cluster or *wheel* of energy. In fact, the word 'chakra' means wheel in Sanskrit. There are chakras or energy points all over the body. Our overall well-being, health and vitality can all be affected when even one chakra is underactive or overactive.

For the remainder of this chapter, we focus on seven main chakra points that are commonly referred to in yoga and often seen in chakra images. Interestingly, the majority of these chakra or energy clusters are located in the body in alignment with clusters of nerves known as the *nerve plexus*. As someone who used to be only science-minded, I would dismiss anything that didn't have a specific study attached to it. Through multiple life experiences, studying the chakras and teaching workshops, I have shifted my mindset to acknowledge the value in human experience. Nonetheless, there are parallels between the chakra system and what modern science tells us about the nervous system. Most importantly, I have witnessed profound healing and empowerment from working with the chakra system with regards to choosing happy. Let's dive in.

The seven main chakra points are associated with different colors, elements, crystals, herbs, symbols, sounds, parts of the world, animals, foods and representations. There are specific health issues associated with each chakra, as well as positive and negative aspects or attitudes, and mental and emotional states. Many of the health issues tied to each chakra are associated with organs that are located physically close to where the chakra is said to be. Using techniques, intentions, yoga poses, meditations, colours, essential oils, affirmations, crystals and healing modalities such as reiki, we can access the chakras, creating a platform for healing and a healthy being. Depending on what challenges we may have experienced in our lives, different chakras in the body are said to be impacted.

Chakras develop at different times or ages in our lives. Experiencing a trauma during a particular chakra's age of development can also cause an overactive or underactive chakra. When we work to heal the energy, we bring the chakra back into 'balance', releasing the impact that a particular trauma may have had. What chakra theory would call 'healing' or 'balancing of energy', science may call 'releasing the tension in the fascia tissue' that the initial trauma created. I do not intend to get tied up in labels here.

Releasing tension from the body or helping to shift energy to feel a sense of flow is a great and important way to create space in the mind, body and spirit. When we do this, it creates an even stronger foundation for choosing happy.

As a precursor to this chakra discussion, I emphasize that the description of the chakras in this section are a simplified version for the purposes of this book. There are entire series of books and courses dedicated to the study of chakras and the depth of this philosophy. Chakra theory teaches us that there is a positive and negative aspect to each of these seven chakras. Recognizing and loving all aspects is an important part of choosing happy. When we can understand, learn and grow from our mistakes as well as embrace our negative or 'dark' aspects, we create compassion. With compassion comes the space for more self-acceptance and acceptance of others. In turn, this leads to a greater sense of happiness. We can flourish and excel from our positive or 'light' aspects, which helps us to see where we can use the mind, body and spirit connection to bring us to the happiness we seek.

As a *system* of energy, it is all connected and there is a constant exchange of energy happening. If one chakra is overactive or underactive, it will impact all the others, meaning all chakras are constantly being influenced. Have you ever walked into a room full of people where you don't really know what's going on but you can feel the energy is buzzing? Or in contrast you can feel the energy is heavy even though you don't know what went on before you entered the room? Have you ever felt yourself being affected by this particular energy? Since energy exchange is happening all the time, we must check in with ourselves on a regular basis to keep the chakras in a balanced state. This is important for health and for choosing happy.

Remember, by discussing the chakras, I am not implying they are the be-all-end-all magical way to heal any disease or life trauma. This is simply another facet of the happiness repertoire. Frankly, it has been incredibly powerful for me and others I've worked with in terms of choosing happy. Delving into the work involved with the chakra system will allow for more clarity, connection and ability to choose happiness.

If chakra theory does not resonate with you, simply taking the life lessons that are connected to each one and working to live from that place will feed, strengthen and magnify your ability for choosing happy. It can also help to look at it from a perspective of seeing the deeper meaning within and recognizing the mind-body connection. Any physical ailments addressed under each chakra can cause specific behaviors, thoughts or emotional challenges. Likewise, when stuck in a negative emotional or behavioral pattern, those can cause associated physical ailments. Knowing this is invaluable.

Then exploring some of the chakra questions cultivates a connection to spirit, because we access truth, love and greater connection. Try to side-step getting caught up in semantics with ideas like *chakra* or *spirit*. Look beyond those words and simply explore 'another' aspect of who you are, understanding that it paves the way for healing and choosing happy.

Each chakra has a Sanskrit name and holds a specific meaning. The seven chakras and their Sanskrit names are:

Chakra One: root chakra, Muladhara meaning root or support.

Chakra Two: sacral chakra, Svadhisthansa meaning sweetness.

Chakra Three: solar plexus chakra, Manipura meaning lustrous gem.

Chakra Four: heart chakra, Anahata meaning unstruck.

Chakra Five: throat chakra, Vishuddha meaning purification.

Chakra Six: brow chakra, Ajna meaning command center.

Chakra Seven: crown chakra, Sahasrara meaning thousand fold.

1. Root Chakra

The root chakra is located at the base of the spine at the perineum. This chakra is concerned with our physical identity, survival and sustainability of life. Food, shelter, security as well as the physical manifestation of dreams or desires are important needs for a balanced root chakra. When the root chakra is functioning optimally, we feel grounded, focused and flexible. The shadow aspect of this chakra is fear. If 'other fear', for example, is consuming your life, that can be indicative of an imbalance in root chakra energy.

A balanced root chakra is maintained by fostering healthy connections to ourselves, others and our community. When our safety is compromised, our sense of belonging is under threat or a negative attitude towards receiving life's gifts exists, then the root chakra is impacted, and its functioning is inhibited. If we feel personally threatened, we can become rigid or even violent, causing us to lose compassion for anything that may be undermining our way of life.

Honoring boundaries can create an energy flow towards a healthy lifestyle. If those boundaries are ignored and the energy of creativity is buried away, more anger will be fueled.

Physical signs of a dysfunctional root chakra are weight problems, either obesity or anorexia, hemorrhoids, constipation, sciatica, degenerative arthritis, knee troubles, issues with the teeth, feet problems, kidney issues and autoimmune deficiency.

This is not to suggest that should we heal the root chakra, these issues will go away. However, addressing these from an energetic or spiritual side can certainly support the healing of these maladies.

A sign of being stuck in the root chakra is when we overvalue the physical and have unhealthy attachments to our possessions, traditions and values, or obsessions with how life or even happiness 'should be'.

If you are struggling with one of these physical issues it is valuable on your healing journey to question just how rigid you may be.

Looking at our behaviours when it comes to survival, safety and rigidity can impact our ability for choosing health and happiness. For instance, having issues with hygiene or paying bills late on a regular basis can be the sign of an underactive root chakra.

The root chakra is one of two chakras said to correspond with the adrenals. The adrenal glands are responsible for the release of epinephrine, one of the four main hormones associated with happiness. Epinephrine isn't officially a hormone that stimulates happiness. Rather, it increases our tolerance to pain. Another way to put it is epinephrine decreases our perception of being uncomfortable. Stimulating the release of epinephrine is a powerful tool for choosing happy, because if we are experiencing discomfort and release epinephrine to help decrease that discomfort, choosing happy becomes that much easier.

However, too much epinephrine isn't great either, because that puts our bodies into a constant fight or flight mode. This can cause all kinds of issues, including adrenal fatigue as well as adrenaline addiction. Many of us can be somewhat 'addicted' to adrenaline because of its nature in easing pain and discomfort. Here's the thing: pain is important. It is how our body, mind or spirit communicates that something is wrong. When we ignore pain, the problem continues to grow and becomes more difficult to address compared to if we had paid attention from the beginning. As much as it is uncomfortable pausing to address pain instead of just building a tolerance to it, it is highly important.

Knowing how to relax and reset to give the adrenals a break is necessary for optimal health. Ideally, we want to create a balance of epinephrine release and then recovery. Balance is one of those overused words, but here it is incredibly applicable.

Accessing the Root Chakra

Reflecting on our childhood and exploring beliefs or values we've created around the idea of happiness can help us begin to heal this chakra. Feeling safe, secure and supported on your journey for choosing happy happens through the root chakra.

Negative attitudes or beliefs can cause a deficient root chakra: demonstrating that life isn't worth it, constantly feeling like the victim, lacking trust in the beauty and possibilities of life, feeling instant despair and gloom when presented with life challenges. When these beliefs become so deep-rooted, they can manifest into some of the physical issues listed above. When these negative attitudes are present, they translate into specific beliefs about happiness such as unworthiness, needing to give something up in exchange for happiness, or there being something dark looming around the corner if we allow ourselves happiness.

If this chakra is out of balance, we might have a fixed mindset or picture around exactly what happiness should look like, limiting the abundance of happiness available.

The first step in addressing this chakra imbalance is getting quiet and asking yourself if you believe you can be happy. Then probe further.

Does your idea of happiness exist outside of you?

Are you willing to be flexible and embrace change?

Are you worthy of happiness?

Is there something you have to do or complete before you can be happy?

Being aware of these beliefs is a great place to start. Beliefs come from somewhere; once we realize they aren't true, we can begin to do the work to unlearn them. I don't want to oversimplify the efforts required, because it can be extremely challenging indeed. However, it isn't impossible and it's *never* too late.

Root chakra energy shifts each time we state what we want out of life. When we make positive affirmations such as "I deserve the life I want" or "I deserve health, joy and stability," we expand our perspective beyond limiting beliefs that happiness is available to others but not ourselves. When our beliefs go from a limited perspective of expecting punishment or harsh consequences to potential and possibility, the root chakra begins to flourish.

I grew up in a home of sometimes brutally harsh consequences that instilled a powerful fear of stepping outside the box or going against the grain. Fear of consequences was so deeply ingrained in me that at times I found myself afraid of any consequence whether it was a good consequence for something I had done well or a not-so-great consequence for a mistake. As I grew older, that fear began to hold me back. It would take me ages to get started on something I was passionate about, even if I knew I was good at it, because *what if I get it wrong?* My mother passing away when I was seven most certainly had an impact. The truth I created was that no matter how much I loved her, behaved well or did what I was told, she still died; life offers harsh consequences no matter what.

Sometimes when something so traumatic happens in childhood, we make it our fault or believe it to be a specific truth about ourselves. Especially when it's something that isn't commonly happening to others around us. We may believe that we must have done something wrong or life simply needs to punish us. This was mine. When I recognized that I had dreams and sharing *The Many Sides of Happy* philosophy was a priority and passion for me, I knew I would have to overcome my fear of consequences, even fear of success, so I could persevere.

A big part of healing this chakra is letting go of narrow beliefs. Start with letting go of any belief you may still have that happiness is not a choice. Honouring your definition of happiness, being true to who you are and fostering your growth and development all help to balance this chakra. Release the need to seek approval from others, as this will free you from rigid binds and choices based on fear.

Using affirmations such as:

"I am safe"

"I am supported"

"I am strong"

"I am ready"

are powerful in helping to move past this paralyzing 'other fear'.

The colour red is associated with the root chakra, so working with red items and crystals will impact the energy.

Specific yoga practices and physical activity modalities are useful in working with the root chakra too.

Use this or any root chakra yoga practice, as well as root chakra affirmations, for healing in this area.

See Appendix D for The Root Chakra Yoga Practice

2. Sacral Chakra

The sacral chakra is located in the lower abdominal pelvic region below the belly button and two inches into the center of the pelvis. The sacral chakra is associated with wellbeing, abundance, pleasure and sexuality. Although this chakra doesn't govern an organ associated with one of the four main happy hormones, it does correspond with our pleasure centers. Pleasure doesn't create sustainable happiness, but if we hold a belief that we don't deserve the life we want, constantly feel experiences of lack or that people deserve to suffer, the ability to engage fully in happiness is significantly restricted. These types of negative beliefs are affiliated with the second chakra. The shadow aspect of this chakra is guilt.

Other mental and emotional states that could indicate an overactive or underactive sacral chakra are jealousy, lack of hygiene, not feeling good enough or deserving of the life you say you want. These mental and emotional states can physically manifest creating issues in the body. Physical malfunctions include: stiff lower back, fertility issues, kidney or bladder trouble, impotence.

It is often said 99% of disease is associated with stress. When stress isn't addressed, it can cause dis-ease in the physical body. Existing in a state where we believe we deserve to suffer or should feel guilty for anyone or anything can create intense stress. A powerful way to manage stress is to understand where the thoughts or beliefs leading to our distress originate. Healing any beliefs of not being good enough or having somehow been cheated can help alleviate the stress related to the physical malfunctions discussed above. As I mentioned in the discussion of the first chakra, healing the emotional or mental states may not mean the physical malfunction disappears instantaneously. However, because we are biopsychosocial beings, we should include this component into our overall healing process.

Accessing the Sacral Chakra

Similar to the root chakra work, looking back at your childhood can give clues as to what needs to be healed. In particular, development between the ages 7 and 14 can give you an idea of any impact on the sacral chakra. It doesn't only have to be during those ages. Trauma to any of our chakras can occur at any age. However, looking at our past can help us to unravel areas where we are not yet aware that something still has a negative effect or 'takes up space' inside us.

Take a few moments to check in with yourself and ask:

> *Are you willing to give yourself breaks from the daily hustle?*
>
> *Do you believe you deserve the things and experiences in life you say you want?*
>
> *Do you carve out time every day to laugh or feel joy?*

Sacral chakra underactivity or overactivity can show up in negative attitudes such as not being worthy of the life we say we want or not feeling like we deserve to experience even the simplest pleasure. This translates into unhappiness, misery and a lack of joy. It can also turn into venomous attitudes and projecting guilt onto others for not improving our life experiences. There is often a victim mentality where our happiness is others' responsibility and a lack of self-empowerment. A rigid attitude can cut us off from the flow of life, happiness and pleasure.

Affirmations are a helpful way to shape and impact our attitude. Here are few suggestions for Sacral Chakra affirmations.

> "I take the time to enjoy all the beauty and pleasure that life has to offer"
>
> "Laughter and joy are a priority each and every day"
>
> "I am deserving of joy, pleasure and ease"

Moving through a sacral chakra practice will help to ease tension, restricted movement and rigidity in the body that can be created from unexpressed emotions buried deep into the muscles, tendons and fascia. When those emotions and feelings are expressed or experienced, we let go physically of damaging stress.

See Appendix E for Sacral Chakra Yoga Practice

3. Solar Plexus Chakra

The solar plexus is said to be located above the stomach and just below the sternum. The solar plexus corresponds with feelings of self-worth, willpower, self-esteem, and freedom of personal choice. Balancing this chakra is about letting go of anger, educating ourselves or increasing knowledge, exercising our willpower to overcome particular challenges, connecting with love, being able to laugh at ourselves and taking care of ourselves. The shadow aspect of the solar plexus is shame, a feeling many of us can relate to that presents as an uneasy feeling in our gut.

The solar plexus is also said to be the home of the ego. Our ego can often get fixated on an idea of power over or power under, instead of connecting with the actual power that matters: personal power, the ability to show up as the truest version of ourselves. There is a common idea around getting rid of our ego and that isn't necessarily the most valuable approach for choosing happy. Instead, it's about managing our ego and being mindful of not taking power from others or readily giving away our own power.

Some physical health issues associated with this chakra are digestive disorders, diabetes, indigestion, gallstones, ulcers and hepatitis. If you happen to struggle with any of these health issues, work with the solar plexus chakra. The solar plexus corresponds with the GI tract where 80-90% of the feel-good hormone serotonin is found. As with any of the chakras, working with the solar plexus can have a powerful impact on our happiness.

Accessing the Solar Plexus

Reflect on values or beliefs established between the ages of 14 and 21 about who we are and what we think we are capable of can be a great indicator of how the solar plexus has been impacted. Taking the time to recognize if those values and beliefs are still true today can help with healing and rebalancing our energy. If they are still true, that is great. If they aren't, we need to let go and set 'new personal rules'.

For any of the chakras, but especially in the area of the solar plexus and personal power, questions can help bring deeper insight and understanding to whether our core beliefs are healthy.

Here are some questions for self-reflection:

Are you able to connect with and acknowledge anything in your life that you are proud of achieving?

Do you feel confident to make changes in your life for choosing happy?

Can you communicate to others in a way that sets firm healthy boundaries for you?

Do you recognize your personal power of choice?

Do you choose to show up as who you really are at all times?

In order to move forward from beliefs that may not serve us, we can use affirmations. Helpful affirmations for the solar plexus are:

"I am worthy of health, love and happiness."

"I choose a life that is best for me and who I know I am."

"I am connected to my personal power, and make choices for the good of myself and others."

A yoga practice filled with twists, core work and some heat is a great way to access this chakra area. The element associated with the solar plexus is fire, so a nice fired-up practice is certainly impactful.

See Appendix F for Solar Plexus Chakra Yoga Practice

4. Heart Chakra

The heart chakra is located in the middle of the chest and is associated with compassion, unity, peace and love. If there is a malfunction, related physical issues include asthma, pneumonia, high blood pressure, angina, heart and lung disease. Emotionally, if this chakra is impacted, we may fear love (giving or receiving), which restricts our ability for joy, health or positivity, blocking our heart from feeling happy. In choosing happy, we must have an open heart.

To access this chakra, the best course to take is to love, to participate in anything that makes our heart sing, to feel alive, to be with people we love and to let ourselves love them and be loved in return.

Fear of losing the ones we love can sometimes be incredibly overwhelming and make us hold back. Let's face it. The pain of loss can be so deep and intense, it seems too much to bear. If we allow this fear to take over, the heart chakra becomes blocked; we have already lost the love.

Once, I walked into an amazing store with crystals and angel cards and all this other cool spiritual stuff. From behind the desk, a woman looked up and addressed me, "My dear, your heart chakra is completely blocked." I had no idea what that meant at that time. I thought she was insane. Yet inside, I was moving through a time where I felt resentful of love. On this particular day, the grief I felt over my mother's death and my father's brain damage was suffocating me to the point where I couldn't see straight. My chest felt like an elephant was sitting on it. I had communicated none of this to her; she simply knew by being in my presence.

Eventually, by doing the inner work to learn to love others deeply again and let them love me, as well as facing my grief, I can feel my 'happy heart' once more. Accessing my heart chakra was powerful in my journey in choosing happy.

In Ambika Wauters' book, *The Complete Guide to Chakras*, she discusses the heart chakra having two components: an outer protective layer and the inner heart. Anatomically, the heart has the pericardium, which is the sac that surrounds the heart and the heart itself. The outer layer of this chakra or as Wauters puts it 'the protector of the heart' is there as a guard. It keeps the heart safe from negative thoughts and harmful criticism that can corrode its innocence. This strong protective layer is maintained through healthy boundaries that support our personal growth and wellbeing.

The internal heart itself is kept healthy through connecting to the gift of love within and respecting the hearts of others. Spending quiet time alone, with nature and with loving positive people helps to keep this component of the heart chakra balanced. Forgiving the past and making space in our hearts to see the beauty and gifts of life help to heal and fuel happiness. The age of resonance for the heart chakra is between 21 and 28.

Accessing the Heart Chakra

Simply teaching ourselves to prioritize and connect with love feeds the needs of this chakra. Making decisions for ourselves and for our lives from a place of love not fear (even though that can be the harder decision) is important in fueling this chakra. Reflecting on our definition of love and asking ourselves to live and love according to this definition is extremely powerful.

Moving through these questions related to the heart chakra, you can gain more insight, and move closer to sustainable joy and happiness.

Do you have a sense of love for yourself, others, nature, animals and life itself?

Are you willing to forgive the past and those who may have hurt you?

Do you prioritize creating and connecting to peace in your life?

Are you willing and able to make changes to create more peace in your life when necessary?

Do you allow deep connections with yourself and others?

Do you prioritize making time to experience joy and do what makes your heart happy on a regular basis?

How could you bring more joy into your life?

Finally, there are affirmations you can repeat that can help with the process of connection, forgiveness, love and joy.

"I honor myself and others. I choose love."

"I choose to fuel the joy that resides within."

"I am filled with love, joy and peace."

"I release the hurt that holds me back and make space for love, happiness and peace."

See Appendix G for Heart Chakra Yoga Practice

5. Throat Chakra

The fifth chakra is located in the throat area and corresponds with communication, creativity and integrity. What we say to others as well as to ourselves in terms of kindness, truth, lies, gossip, love or hate will all impact the balance of this chakra. Speaking up for ourselves in a balanced way with healthy boundaries can help this chakra flourish. Swallowing our feelings down, not sticking up for something we believe in or not honouring yes when we mean yes or no when we mean no will all impact this chakra in a negative way.

Physical malfunctions related to the throat chakra include laryngitis, stiff neck, hearing issues, issues with the teeth, thyroid problems and colds.

Emotionally, a blocked or impacted throat chakra can look like the inability to speak or stand up for oneself. Lying, substance abuse and gossip all can have a negative impact on this chakra.

The age of resonance for the throat chakra is said to be between 28 and 35. Interestingly, this is often the age when we learn to stick up for ourselves and our beliefs. Coincidence? Who's to know for sure?

Accessing the Throat Chakra

Integrity cultivates an environment of respect, which is profound for healing. When we are respected by ourselves and others, choosing happy is that much easier. Holding ourselves accountable to be as honest and truthful as possible helps to balance this energy. Likewise, nurturing and exploring our creative sides and bringing about as many opportunities as possible for expression is also beneficial for this chakra. Gossip is damaging to ourselves and to others, so we must be mindful of how we talk about others and operate from a place of integrity.

Paying attention to our feelings is one way to get in touch with our inner truth. Connecting with how we feel about our lives, the people in it, the directions we are taking are all powerful ways to balance out this chakra. It's a lot easier to speak from our truth when we are actually connected to it. The throat chakra is associated with communication, which isn't always about speaking up or speaking out. It can also be about listening and being quiet to witness subtle messages coming through (such as body language, energy levels or enthusiasm). It's also about listening to others' truth and wisdom, as that can help us to grow and connect deeper to our own. This may look like opposite views to our own, being able to listen with an open mind and advocating from a healthy perspective is important to balance this chakra.

Questions you can ask to dig a little deeper:

> *Are you open in your communication?*
>
> *Do you say what's on your mind or how you feel (with tact not cruelty!) on a consistent basis?*
>
> *Do you speak your truth from a place of compassion for yourself without needing to take away another person's power?*
>
> *Do you currently operate from a place of integrity?*
>
> *Do you take time to explore and express your creative side on a regular basis?*

Positive affirmations are exceptional for the throat chakra, because speaking in a positive manner brings more healing to this particular area.

Here are a few suggested throat chakra affirmations.

> *"I communicate my feelings easily from a place of honesty and integrity."*
>
> *"I am willing to listen with a sense of openness."*
>
> *"I create opportunities to connect with my creativity and to express it."*

Singing is a great way to heal and release trapped energy too! (Car pool karaoke, anyone?) Different forms of communication, especially public speaking and writing, fuel and balance this chakra.

See Appendix H for Throat Chakra Yoga Practice

6. Brow Chakra

The brow chakra is located just above eye level in the center of the head. The primary role of this chakra is the health of the mind. When we have a healthy mind, the physical health of the body also improves.

Speaking with my doctor when I received the all clear from my cancer experience, I expressed how fortunate I felt compared to so many others. As we discussed my recovery, she told me my positive attitude had played a major part in my experience. I remember my surgeon coming into my hospital room. As I greeted him with a smile, he said, "You don't look like you belong here! Time to go home."

The brow chakra is associated with the pineal gland which is often called the 'master gland' of the body. It is called this because it secretes a hormone that regulates the other glands in the body. Positive thoughts have a powerful influence on this gland. Thoughts that are restricting in terms of our self-worth inhibit the ability for this gland to function optimally. It is important to acknowledge that indeed there is more at play than just positive thoughts with our physical heath; however, it is arrogant and dangerous to discount the contribution that thinking in a positive and supportive manner can play.

Malfunction of the brow chakra, also known as the 'third eye', can show up as depression, migraines, issues with vision, inability to learn, confusion and strokes. Connection to imagination, internal wisdom, intuition and cultivating understanding all support the energy of this chakra. Should you experience any of these physical symptoms, connecting to any of the of the behavioral or emotional states listed can help with healing.

The brow chakra is associated with ages 35 to 42.

Accessing the Brow Chakra

The brow chakra flourishes with positive thoughts and languishes in negativity. Positive affirmations are incredibly important in healing the brow chakra. Work on the self and letting go of harmful or untrue thoughts or beliefs keeps this chakra thriving. Healthy boundaries that honor our acceptance of ourselves are of the utmost importance for the health of this chakra.

To gain a little more insight as to your inner sense of where you thrive, answer these few brow chakra questions.

Are you able to and do you turn inward to connect to your personal wisdom regarding decisions that foster happiness in your life?

Do you listen to and receive wisdom from others' life experiences and what they offer you?

Do you set healthy boundaries around those who may be manipulative and lack understanding for who you are or what is in your best interest?

Do you make time to learn about issues that are meaningful and important to you?

Do you allow yourself time to imagine your greatest life, filled with financial abundance, health, vitality and being loved for who you are?

Do you respect and listen to your gut feelings or intuition?

The following are a few brow chakra affirmations to try:

"I connect to my inner wisdom and choose to listen for direction on my path to happiness."

"I am open to the limitless possibilities for happiness."

"I gather wisdom and knowledge to grow and heal."

See Appendix I for Brow Chakra Meditation

7. Crown Chakra

The seventh chakra is located at the top of the head. Similar to the sixth chakra, the crown chakra is connected to the pineal gland and benefits from positive thoughts and attitudes. This plays a powerful role and influences the pineal gland to release hormones that create happy experiences. When this chakra is open or thriving, it brings a positive attitude and outlook on life. Greater self-acceptance is established, as well as compassion for life.

Balance and openness of this chakra brings about an awareness to a sense of purpose for life. As this chakra heightens our ability to see the 'bigger picture', it brings a greater sense of perspective. The emotional state of bliss is associated with the crown chakra.

Malfunctions in this chakra can show up as confusion, an inability to learn, depression, nervous disorders and insomnia.

Emotional malfunction can express itself as being trapped in the ego with manipulative and arrogant behaviours. There is also a lack of recognition to being connected to the world and people around us. There exists a 'me versus everything else' type attitude instead of an understanding of 'we'.

Accessing the Crown Chakra

The crown chakra opens through connectivity and positivity. It requires a significant period of time spent alone, in peace and quiet, with a focus on self-inquiry. Stepping away from our material desires and instead tapping into our sense of purpose or understanding our 'why' opens this chakra. The highest state of this chakra is enlightenment, where we gather the understanding of our connection to all things.

Here a few questions that can help you explore the seventh chakra.

Are you willing to see or learn a different perspective with an open mind?

Are you able to see the deeper meaning in encounters or experiences?

Do you feel you have a sense of purpose?

Here are your crown chakra affirmations.

"I love and accept who I am and see the beauty that exists within me."

"I appreciate all the gifts that surround me and contribute to my life."

"I am grateful for the beauty of nature and the earth. I take care of it to the best of my ability."

See Appendix J for Crown Chakra Meditation

It is possible to revisit any or all of the chakras to continue exploring, clearing out space and connecting throughout a lifetime of choosing happy. So often I am told by workshop participants that they never would have thought to explore these questions, yet they experience profound clarity when they do. Chakra work clarifies and unpacks the clutter that no longer serves you. If this brief introduction to the chakras has made an impact on you, I highly recommend researching and exploring them further.

CHAPTER 13

Many Sides of Me

Eventually, unhealed experiences that have negatively impacted us will take up space and impact all aspects of our life. Indeed, we are capable of pretending everything is perfectly fine. Many would even argue this can be necessary at times. However, the person we are on the inside is still impacted and it's important to be aware of that. We are not impermeable, and those emotions don't just go away.

One way we can look at this is that *one side* of us has been impacted. In survival mode, we may cope by seeing that we have *many sides* to who we are and what we do. Therefore, even though one side of our life may have been impacted, we can create an awareness and choose to hold space for positive experiences in other areas. Challenging situations do not have to stay all-consuming. When life takes a turn and drop-kicks us in the head, it is oh-so easy to forget about being happy. In the thick of a situation or amidst the initial shock of a circumstance or trauma, we can consciously 'park' the challenge for a short period, as a survival mechanism.

In Western culture, there is an expectation that when we show up at work we leave all our personal stuff at the door. I understand where this standard comes from, as it would be difficult to get any work done if we were constantly pouring emotions all over the place. However, what we need to understand is the same person who has been impacted by something personally is the same person who is trying to walk through the office door. The divorce, the debt, the family health issues, the stress, and the related grief, sadness or anxiety don't just disappear.

The point I make here is this: if we don't address the buried down feelings or experiences from the past or even present, they will eventually seep into other aspects of our life where we may not want them.

Many 'sides' of you exist, but they are not *totally separate*. There is a binding component in the middle and that component is you. It's not only valuable from a healing perspective to understand that many sides of you exist; it is also important if you want to thrive. Honouring these different sides of who you are will foster a greater ability to choose happy. Engaging in all aspects of who you are will behave as a stress buffer. How? If there happens to be a crisis or challenge in one area of your life, you can access other areas to ground yourself.

A yoga student and now dear friend of mine had a father who was admitted to a nursing home at just 45 years old, a marriage that fell a part through infidelity and a mother diagnosed with breast cancer only a year later. My friend had plenty of reasons to be unhappy and there were definitely times when it was all she could do to keep herself from crumbling. The fear and sadness brewing over her mother's diagnosis overwhelmed her. However, at work, she was still able to laugh, connect with others, and in her words "feel genuinely happy." At her workplace, she recognized that she could find the opportunity to tune into her happiness. Her strategy? Making a conscious effort to not bring her home situation into work. She made a choice. She didn't talk about her home challenges at work unless she needed to ask her manager for time off. Her work was a buffer. It was another side of her life.

This is an extremely valuable coping tool when life becomes overwhelming; having reminders that happiness does exist in other areas of our lives will help.

A note of caution... When we experience that sense of happiness, freedom and escape in one particular role in our lives, we can sometimes immerse ourselves so heavily in that role that we create an avoidance pattern. There is a fine line with survival mode between immersing ourselves in a particular side of our lives just to get through the day and letting it completely take over so we avoid other aspects of life. This can lead us down a dangerous path towards some unhealthy behaviours so it's important to stay mindful. Be present in your sense of enjoyment and pleasure. Let it feed your soul to the fullest. Fill your cup! Then recognize that you may have to set something aside for now, but in order to create sustainable happiness, you will have to process and heal it at some point. As we have already learned, unhealed issues will eventually seep into other areas of our lives.

My same yoga friend who compartmentalized also went back and did the work. Just like her, check in and do what is required to heal those wounds. Like her, you may even become an incredible example of what it means to live a life choosing happy.

Action time:

You are going to see a few different versions of this wheel throughout the chapter. The first version I want you to work with is simply the 'many sides of what I do' version. In each section of the circle, fill in the different hats you wear or all the different roles you fulfil.

Examples could be: mother, daughter, cousin, sister, co-worker, boss, coach, cleaner, chef, friend, etc.

Many Sides of What I Do Wheel

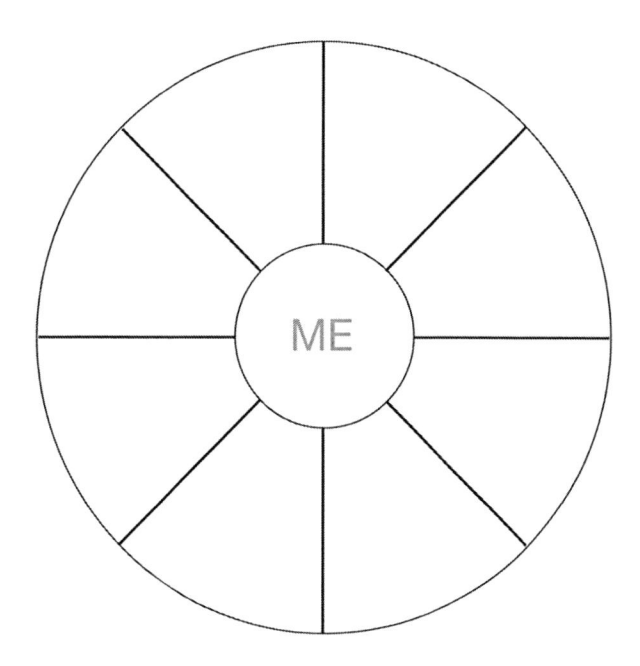

Once you have established what you do, take a moment to step back and simply observe. It's pretty amazing to see all the different ways you spend your time.

Now take another moment to reflect on your definition of happiness that you wrote back in the Defining Happy chapter. When you look at all your roles, is your definition of happiness included? Be careful to resist the temptation to dive in and think of all the ways you need to 'fix' any components or immediately set goals to meet some sort of 'ideal happiness' construct. Doing more or fixing something is not always the answer.

When observing this Many Sides of What I Do Wheel, see how often you are challenged to make choices and how those choices impact so many areas of life.

Now that you have spent time just hanging out with all these 'sides' of you, answer these questions:

> *Where do you connect with your definition of happiness the most out of all those roles? And where do you connect the least?*
>
> *Are there certain areas where you could make different choices that would support or include your definition of happiness more?*
>
> *Are there certain areas that could use more time and energy compared to others?*
>
> *Are there certain areas you need to connect with right now to remember what happiness feels like?*

There is no right or wrong answer to these questions. Happiness is about you and your needs.

Where we need to allocate our attention, where we need to grow or where we may need to let go will fluctuate constantly. I am definitely not suggesting immediate life-altering changes either. It's important to recognize we can't do all this work at once. It is way too much pressure and could seriously chuck you into a healing crisis. Taking small baby steps and doing things bit by bit can be unbelievably difficult for some of us. Yet this is how we do this work.

Look at the small shifts you could make in the sections where you don't see your definition of happiness at all. What would allow more of your perspective of happiness to be included? This exercise isn't a one-stop experience. You can go back to it again and again. Setting new intentions, tweaking where needed or simply checking in and observing how flipping awesome you really are, these are all possibilities for gradual change.

Once you have established what you do and how your definition of happiness can be worked into those experiences, look next at who you are. In terms of choosing happy, it's important to get know yourself, the real human you.

Once, my physician explained to me how interesting she found it when she asked people to tell her about themselves. The first thing people always talked about was what they do, she told me. I could understand why people respond to the 'tell me about yourself' question with what they do. And it's cool if you do that too. What's important, though, is for you to know that's what you do, not who you are. I want to be very clear here so read this slowly. *What you do is not who you are!*

Who Are You?

You might teach, so you work in education. You might help people with their finances, so you work in financial planning. Maybe you can fix cars so you work as a mechanic. You might work from home, have your own business, run a company, work in healthcare, have children…

But who *are* you?

So often, we identify with our work or a particular role we play in our lives. And as long as that is going well, we will be happy, right? But what if that role changes? At some point, it most likely will. This is how life moves forward. If we have placed our identity in that role and there happens to be a change, it can create an extreme experience of rupture. People report feeling lost, confused, unimportant or having no sense of value at times when these changes occur. The person inside is still there — the 'you' — and absolutely you still matter, regardless of what has changed. So how do we get to know the real you?

Action time:

How do you get to know more about who you are? It's circle time again. Take a deep breath and turn your focus inward. Start to reflect. Pause and write down the different aspects of what you know about yourself.

Are you creative? Are you logical? Are you energized by people? Are you energized by quiet? Are you sensitive? Are you quick-witted, patient, easily frustrated, curious...?

Many Sides of my Personality Wheel

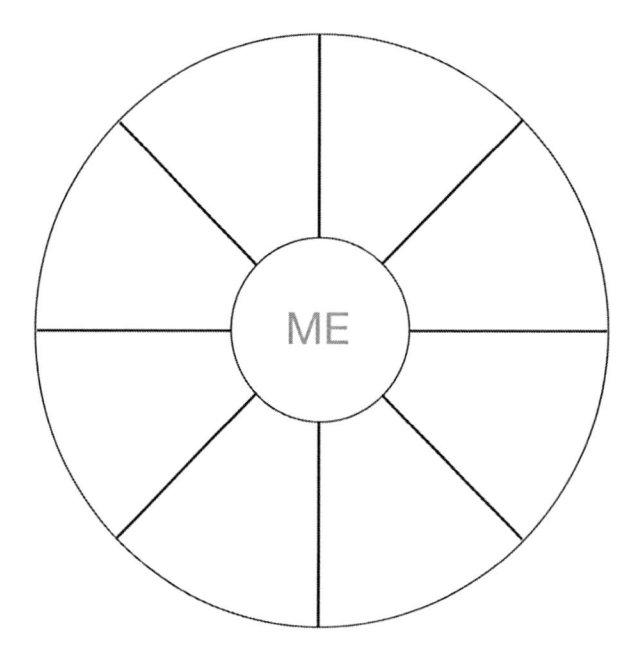

When you fill out this wheel, be sure not to judge. Who you are is perfect! It also evolves. Who you are today might look different in one, two or ten years' time.

Understanding, accepting and even working with these aspects of ourselves is an empowering part of choosing happy, because you are being truthful and honouring who you are. You are connecting to you. What's amazing is you may notice how these aspects of who you are already show up in what you do. However, you may also notice possibilities of where you can show even more of these sides of yourself in your work.

When I began to honour who I was in my parenting role, a massive shift happened. For a long time, I tried to operate from a place of who I thought I should be as a mom. I read tons of books and tried to be what the book said I was supposed to be. When I stepped back and honoured myself, I let my parenting evolve from that place. And the resistance I felt inside and from my family were huge! Yet I am grateful for this process as I also figured out who I am not. My husband laughs whenever someone asks him for new baby parenting advice. He'll say, "Sure, read the books. But be sure you don't lose who you are as a person and parent in the process." So true.

In short, knowing who we are means tapping into and taking note of what felt right and what didn't. 'Failure' is so not a bad thing in this sense, because it helps you know what doesn't feel like you or make you happy. This can be just as valuable as knowing what does feel like you and makes you happy. Life challenges can also be valuable here, because we often get to know an aspect of ourselves in those defining moments when there is no energy or time to pretend to be someone else.

What Do You Enjoy?

After looking at the aspects of how you might describe your personality or your traits, you can start to think about activities that aren't just work or parenting, but what you enjoy doing that feeds what you know about yourself.

When my bestie was having her second baby at home, the midwives were walking her through a relaxation visualization. They began talking about being on the beach, on the sand, by the water. She stopped the midwives and asked if they could change the visualization from the being on the beach to walking through the container store, because organizing was an activity that made her happy and relaxed. She knew this made her feel good and she owned it. Now, the container store might not be everyone's typical happy place, but that didn't matter because it was hers.

The same applies to you when thinking about what makes you feel happy. This is such a helpful exercise because we can forget what we used to like to doing when we were younger, or become so caught up in work and life that we no longer make time for what brings us joy. Remembering activities we loved and then doing them doesn't mean we abandon our responsibilities, but it does mean carving out time for what feels good to us.

Action time:

It's time for another wheel. This time you're going to fill in the activities that make you happy, alive, or connected to the real you when you do them.

Here are some examples:

- *fishing*
- *running*
- *reading*
- *yoga*
- *cooking (oh I wish I loved cooking more)*
- *cleaning*
- *organizing*
- *golf*
- *playing an instrument*
- *kitchen dance parties*
- *essential oils.*

Many Sides of What I Love to Do Wheel

You name it. What you put down is totally up to you. These are all joys that contribute to the 'you' in the middle. They are the activities that fill your cup.

Once you get started, it can be difficult to stop! This exercise serves as a reminder that there is so much you can connect with to feel happy. The key is they have to be meaningful to you. Who cares what anyone else thinks? If it brings you joy and is not harmful to you or anyone else, it's time to include more of it in your life.

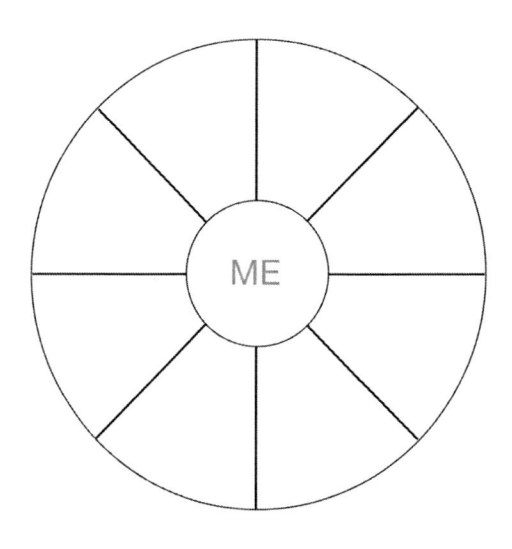

What to Do with Your Wheels

These wheels are designed to help you gain an understanding of all that makes up who you are. At the end of the day, there aren't enough words in any language to embody and describe you completely. You are the circle in the middle. And all these words and definitions are merely parts of your life experience, not the whole.

Embracing the many sides of happy means loving and honouring the 'me' in the middle just because. You *deserve* love and happiness. Just because. Full stop. Not for what you do. Not for any of the roles you listed in any of these wheels. But simply because you are you. These wheels are designed to help you dig a little deeper, connect a little further and understand who you are, but they are not the be all end all of you.

You are you. You deserve love. No ties, no strings attached, no contract to sign, no personality assessment. You, as you are, deserve love.

As we look at all the sides that impact us and what can happen to those sides of ourselves, see it just as it is: stuff that happened, not stuff that gets to hurt you, not stuff that convinces you that you are undeserving of happiness. Know you can make choices within these many sides to honour the you in the middle. Choosing happy doesn't stand a chance if you prioritize avoidance and pushing through, dismissing the you in the middle.

When you heal or acknowledge and let go of past hurt that impacted any of these sides, it's amazing how present stress problems diminish, because you have more space for who you are. Yes, present circumstances can still cause stress. However, your ability to deal with and process it is drastically different when you have that little bit more room to pause, gain perspective and authentically show up as yourself.

Deciding How You Want to Show Up

Sometimes you may want to avoid truly being the you in the middle of those wheels, because you've made mistakes in the past, or been mean, or said cruel words, and you may ashamed of that person. To be crystal clear, this work is not an entitlement to go around being a total jerk or acting self-righteous or thinking you are above making mistakes. It's not about shaming where you came from either. It's also not about inflicting harm or searching for power over others. None of these equal choosing happy. Behaving that way might give you an ego boost, which may feel good in the moment, but choosing to take away others' power to serve your agenda is not true sustainable happiness.

Okay, so what if we've been the biggest jerk in the room sometime in the past? What do we do about that? First, it's super important to admit it to ourselves and know that we are capable of being that person.

I cringe at some of the ways I behaved when I was younger. I gossiped, I judged, and I name-called. I have certainly been the biggest jerk in the room in my past.

Recognizing and admitting this allows me to see that I am human and can grow from that behaviour, because I am repulsed by it. Knowing I am capable of it allows me to choose how I want to show up now in a way that honours who I am.

I promise you this: operating from a place of compassion, love, generosity and healthy boundaries is definitely where I want to show up from now on. What's more is this feels like me, so I feel happier when I behave this way. Do I still get angry? Absolutely. However, using that anger towards positive change versus negative bashing aligns with choosing happy. Choosing happy doesn't mean bending over backwards for other people. It means saying yes when you mean yes and saying no when you mean no. You need to be true to you.

Using these wheels as a check-in can also help us see where we are making choices that keep us stuck, prevent us from moving forward, and stop us from experiencing more happiness. Stepping back to reflect on these different sides and creating a connection with yourself – now, here, today – can be an incredible way of gaining perspective and a reminder to yourself that you matter!

Navigating these different sides is part of the process. People may say, "I am really happy in *this* particular part of my life, but over here, not so much." You may also hear, "Having this in my life is what got me through the hard times."

Sometimes one particular side needs to be addressed. Sometimes acceptance is in order and you must let go of the power that one side holds over you. Sometimes things can't be changed right now. Only you know the truth around your need for acceptance or your need for change.

Be grateful for your different sides. If you're feeling overwhelmed, step back and take a deep breath. Pause and smile at all that is you. You do not have to be or do everything at once. It can be challenging to accept your humanity, all that makes up who you are and all that you are connected to, because there is an immense amount of responsibility attached to that. However, there is also so much beauty, potential for growth, opportunity for love and possibility for happiness. Often, it just comes down to how you view it.

To put it simply, choosing happy requires a certain perspective. Zooming out to look at our lives can bring the perspective we need to see — whether we need happiness or healing — then connect to happiness either way.

I'll never forget walking into my bathroom one day to see my husband standing naked in front of the mirror checking himself out. He stuck out his belly, pulled in his belly and flexed his muscles. Then he turned to me and said, "You know what, Mieka?" Dramatic pause... Me holding back the unhelpful sarcastic remarks... "All I see is potential," he said. Even as someone who believes in positivity, those weren't quite the thoughts that came to mind, but he was 100% right. If nothing else, choosing happy asks you to be willing to see the potential.

CAUTION: It is possible to continue to rehash and revisit old wounds over and over, ending up trapped in the healing process or 'victim mode'. Tony Robbins once said we can be victimized but we are not victims. This description implies that we can lose our awareness of our power of choice when we identify as a victim. In this space, we quickly forget to forge ahead and live our lives.

If your definition of happy isn't included in one area of your life, maybe it's time to let that part of life go and move on. There is no way to know what that looks like for every person. The only one who truly knows if more healing is needed or it's time to move on is you. To get that sense of clarity, it may take some effort to peel back the internal layers and connect to your intuition or personal wisdom. However, your next steps are there and it's possible.

At the beginning of this chapter, I talked about a friend who was able to leave her personal problems at the door when she went to work. This friend always expresses just how grateful she is for having different outlets available to her, so she never forgets happiness exists. When she was experiencing challenge in some areas, it reminded her to keep going and to live her life.

If we find ourselves without another side where we can make space for happiness, we may be capable of creating one. How? By going back to the Happiness Groundwork Tools and seeing how we can incorporate more of them. Perhaps there's an exercise group, meditation session, cooking class or community you want to join where you can find relief, create connections and discover another side of you. All this work takes time, so be patient. Keep diving into your groundwork and know you are putting in effort that will pay off.

Now that you've looked at the many sides of happy, there is one more piece to the puzzle. There always is, isn't there? Wouldn't it be amazing if we could just do the work once and be done? Read a book, answer a couple of questions, understand a few theories, and we're all done and good to go; I'd sign up for that. There is a final aspect we must explore and that's coming up in the next section: all about having the courage to step into a happy life and actually live it.

PART THREE: LIVING HAPPY

Life Lessons and Choosing Happy Reminders

Take action to be happy. This may seem like a redundant statement, but so many people struggle with simply allowing themselves to be happy. Healing, processing and understanding your definition of happiness are all incredibly important. However, a time comes where you just have to live it.

Enough with the research, the digging, the search for another meaning, the rehashing of stories. It's amazing how long we can get stuck in this phase! Eventually, we have to step out of that effort and allow ourselves to indulge in what makes us happy, to give ourselves permission to feel and be happy, no strings attached, just pure joy.

Having the opportunity to embrace the goal we have been striving for all this time – in this case happiness – is when we can struggle most. Yet the whole point is to be it, live it, love it, feel it as deeply as you can, celebrate it in the way that makes sense to you. Honour your way of choosing happy. There is no destination with this stuff. You will be challenged to choose happy on a daily (even hourly!) basis. The great part is you can. It might take practice, but what a fun practice it is! Right now, go do it! Try your happiness on!

The final part of this book contains life lessons and powerful ah-ha moments that allowed me to find deeper connection to my understanding of choosing happy. They act as little reminders allowing me to see so many more sides of happiness or wake-up calls for those moments where I'm flailing or lost. These can be read in the order they are presented, or if there is a theme that speaks to you, feel free to jump to that section.

I look back at these lessons all the time, because it's so easy to get distracted or pulled in another direction that no longer serves me in choosing happy. Every time, they make me pause and reflect. They allow me to find my feet again on the choosing happy path.

CHAPTER 14

F**k It!

Self-explanatory really! Sometimes, in order to choose happy, you just have to have the ability to say "f**k it!"

I believe that you will know intuitively when you have to draw a line, walk away and just say "f**k it!" Some things will consume far too much of your time, energy and attention. Are you letting these things take up so much space in your life because you value them and they create purpose? Or are you operating on a 'should' and 'supposed to' policy? Take a moment to reflect. It might be time to simply say "f**k it" to a particular situation and move on. Done and done! Next!

Anyone can get caught in a constant obsession with healing or a spiral of avoidance. Either way, learning the art of knowing when to just say "f**k it" is a valuable choosing happy strategy.

If really stuck or overwhelmed, I encourage you to write a f**k-it list. Here's how that valuable tool works. First, don't over think it. Pause and ask yourself: *is there anything right now where I could simply say "f**k it"?* Don't try to find anything. Simply say "f**k it" to what comes up and move on. Try it now. Get out a piece of paper and let it flow. Whatever comes to mind that no longer needs or deserves your attention, say it out loud and then follow it up with "f**k it!"

This exercise creates a load of space, releases the ruminating and supports another perspective. And of course, it makes room for choosing happy.

CHAPTER 15

Discipline and Consistency

Hear the word 'discipline' and think 'punishment'? You're not alone, but that is not my meaning here. I mean putting in the hard work, committing, sticking to something even when it's difficult, or something else feels easier or more enticing.

Choosing happy requires an incredible amount of discipline. Depending on our circumstances, we may not be in a positive environment that supports our choosing happy initiative. But as we learned earlier, circumstances only play a 10% role in happiness. However, that doesn't mean they don't impact us or require some conscious effort and thought to overcome in order to connect with the intentional activities that will contribute to our happiness.

Shocking news or disappointing situations in our home life can become front and center of our world. If happiness is what we want, it will require an exceptional amount of discipline to take the necessary action to participate in intentional happy activities. Exercise, eating well, journaling, meditation, these all take a certain amount of discipline to do on a regular basis. It isn't easy, but it's totally worth it.

You will get distracted, you will be tired, you will get frustrated, you may feel like the only one who is working on happiness. These require you to dig in deeper than you ever thought possible to stay committed to how you want to live your life.

So how do you stay disciplined?

Surround yourself with like-minded people whenever you can. Positivity spreads. If you are encircled by inspiring people, it is that much easier to maintain the required discipline to support your happy journey.

Be mindful of the TV and social media you watch or consume. There are many incredible online groups and pages with tips to support you on this journey. When you watch TV or go onto a social media page, take a moment to be aware of how it makes you feel. If you feel depleted or discouraged after reading or watching something, instead of dwelling in it, switch it off or see if you can come up with an actionable solution to help the situation. It is one thing to be a conscious person who wants to be aware of world events and quite another thing to get absorbed in senseless gossip or constant complaining that fills up your time and space.

Be careful online. Some groups can be supportive and uplifting. Others can be a place for griping, trolling and fueling negativity. That energy will suck your determined discipline right out of your life force. Purge and filter your feeds to display only what serves and supports you. It's important to stay informed. Absolutely, it is. Informed is very different than obsessed and all-consumed. Be aware.

Fill your physical space with reminders, quotes and affirmations. Write them down and post them everywhere. Plan your days. Carve out time to eat the good food, rest, exercise and reflect. If you have a day that doesn't work out, try again tomorrow. Keep coming back to your version of choosing happy again and again and again. The discipline and consistency will begin to add up and create the life you want.

CHAPTER 16

Forgiveness

For some, forgiveness is another f-word. Have you ever heard anyone say: "I will never forget and I will never forgive"? Eventually, being able to forgive someone, a circumstance or yourself is profoundly powerful when it comes to choosing happy.

The definition of 'forgive' according to dictionary.reference.com is *cease to feel resentment against*. I understand wholeheartedly how difficult that process can be. I have heard others say and said myself, "That action or behavior is simply unforgivable." However, as I have learned by moving out of victim mode and choosing happy, the act of forgiveness is freeing and empowering.

Forgiveness needs to apply to both the external person who hurt you in some way and yourself. This also applies to times you spent not choosing happy. I have witnessed many who hold resentment towards themselves for not connecting with their ability to choose happy earlier. Have compassion towards yourself and your choices, if this applies to you. Understand that all of us only know what we know at the time. We are only ready when we are ready. There are times I hate that statement, yet it has rung so true in many instances in my life.

To clarify, forgiveness does not mean you are a doormat. It does not mean you remain in a toxic or harmful situation.

I have had people in my life where the simple mention of their name would make me lose my appetite and have heart palpitations. The idea of forgiving them seemed counterintuitive and totally out of the question. Then I took a course where I had to write a letter to that one person who I just couldn't forgive and include any aspects I was responsible for in the encounter.

To qualify, there are encounters where the person doing the forgiving has absolutely no responsibility in what happened. It is still possible, in their own time, to work towards forgiveness. In other situations, there can be aspects that we are responsible for. These were the situations referred to in the course I was taking.

Initially, I thought this was insane. Clearly, the course instructor could not be talking to me and had no idea what this person had done. However, I decided to embrace the exercise despite my resentment. I managed to scribble down two actions I wasn't proud of while engaging with this person.

After the course, I contacted this person even though we hadn't spoken for two years. I owned my part and I apologized. I didn't receive an apology back, but the beautiful part was I didn't need one. I felt free. I was able to let go.

I also realized that any relationship with this person had to end because it was toxic. I wish this person no harm and hope they enjoy a lovely life. No longer does that particular story or situation hold any power over me. Releasing them gave me so much space. I felt I was in charge. I was liberated. I forgave. For years, I'd played victim to this situation, because it began as a child when my choices were more limited. However, as an adult, I could either continue to play the same re-run in my head or I could see with compassion how this person was a product of their past. The past can shape a person's behavior, I realized. It doesn't mean I *understood* the choices they made, because I didn't, but I was done thinking about it, giving it my energy, wanting revenge.

Forgive, forgive, forgive. Forgiveness is important because anger will eat you alive. Anger is an emotion that, if held on to, doesn't serve anybody. I draw only false power from anger. Where there is anger, happiness cannot thrive.

Forgiveness may take time and require a process all of its own. I would highly recommend working with a trusted professional on this process when *you* are ready. At the end of this chapter, I have included a link to an article on how to begin, as a little guidance in this department can be so valuable.

Remember, too, forgiving someone does not mean they belong in your life or that you condone their actions. That is not the case at all. They just don't get to have your energy anymore. If we become victimized by our circumstances, we remain trapped and disconnected from happiness. One of my favourite quotes reads, "Holding onto anger is like drinking poison and expecting the other person to die." (I am unsure of the original source for this quote)

In order for you to thrive and choose happy, surround yourself with an environment that breeds love. It can take time to change or remove yourself from a toxic situation, but the moment you recognize it for what it is, begin implementing a plan that will serve you and your happiness. Reach out for help and move forward. Be patient with yourself as you move beyond certain circumstances. Each day, even taking a baby step towards where you want to go means you are making a choice, being empowered, refusing to be victim and not blaming someone or something else. You own your choice over your happiness.

> *"The practice of forgiveness has been shown to reduce anger, hurt depression and stress, and leads to greater feelings of hope, peace, compassion and self-confidence. Practicing forgiveness leads to healthy relationships as well as physical health. It also influences our attitude, which opens the heart to kindness, beauty and love."*
>
> (Dr. Fredrick Luskin from learningtoforgive.com)

CHAPTER 17

Calling Out the Excuses

Let's be clear from the outset. Calling out the excuses doesn't apply all the time. It is an action where we need to check in every so often, though, because it will help us in the honesty and integrity department. Sometimes we need compassion, space and time. Sometimes we need to get serious and call ourselves out on the bullsh*t. The only one who knows the right amounts of each is you.

Sometimes what we do, say or think about that stops us choosing happy is, to be frank, just total BS. It's amazing – like, practically a superpower or talent – simply how long we can dwell on and create an entire lifestyle built around excuse after excuse, also known as BS.

Let me qualify this. When I say excuse, I mean thoughts or statements like, "I don't have time to be happy" or "Everyone else gets to be happy and I don't" or "I don't deserve to be happy" or "I will be happy once [insert person] is happy." Excuses, excuses, excuses!

These questions always get interesting responses in my workshops:

Who is responsible for your happiness? (You.)

Can you make someone else happy? (No.)

Can someone else make you happy? (No.)

Yet, there are so many instances when someone is doing 'all the right things', but for whatever reason, they're still unhappy. The person wanting happiness still has to go the final distance of stepping into their happy space. Can others help make it easier or more difficult to be happy? Sure. But at the end of the day, it's down to you.

At a conference with one of my favourite business coaches Natalie MacNeil, I heard the term 'radical personal responsibility' in relation to running your business. And this phrase blew my mind. This is no difference when choosing happy. Take radical personal responsibility and call yourself out wherever you are making excuses in terms of why happiness isn't available right now.

You may not be able to address every problem in this exact moment. However, don't let that turn into ruminating on why you will never be able to be happy or an excuse when you could be taking action in another area of your life. One of my favourite statements is 'not yet' for these purposes. You may be dealing with a crisis, so no, being happy is not working right now, but it's not forever gone. You're just 'not yet' connecting with it.

When you're going down this path, you need to start to break down what you're trying to do into baby steps that allow you to move forward. Maybe start a daily affirmation practice, get outside and walk for ten minutes, or journal for five minutes. Any action you take counts. Instead of making another excuse as to 'why happiness is not available', do something small.

Then focus on and celebrate the fact that you are taking steps in the direction you want to go. (More on the value of celebration later.) The key to this exercise is to stop and listen to what follows when you say or think: *"I am choosing happy."* If something negative follows, if you deem choosing happy impossible, call it out. No judging. Just BS and move on!

It's refreshing when we hear ourselves making an excuse, see it for what it is and realize it's bullsh*t. I taught an entire yoga class around this theme once and the participants all shared how empowering it was to reflect and call out their own excuses without judgment, just being real with themselves.

So where do you begin? Start by making a rule for yourself: no more excuses. Making excuses might allow you to feel a little better about certain circumstances in the moment. They can also create an imaginary buffer that behaves as a guard or protection against whatever the real issue is. When looking for happiness, making excuses is the polar opposite of empowerment. Excuses mean you can't step forward, because you give away your power to move in the direction you want to go.

Action time:

Check in with the excuse, observe and explore it.

Sometimes, we legitimately didn't have a choice over what happened to us or we didn't know better. These cases are obviously not excuses, so checking in on the *evidence* around the belief is valuable.

Take a moment and step outside of your emotional attachment to the excuse or justification to continue the behaviour that is not serving you. It's tough because emotion always overrides logic. Look at the situation from the different angles you are using to stay where you are. Do they all apply? Is the excuse simply work-avoidance or resistance to necessary change?

When doing any of the action items, try to step away from where or who you want to be. Instead, observe the situation at hand. Does it warrant an excuse? Is there anything you *could* do? You might not be able to do something about the situation today, but that doesn't mean you get to wash it away with an excuse either. Notice how often you are using excuses that can you replace with some kind of action.

If you see yourself making certain excuses that seem super lame, be careful to not judge yourself. Initially, self-judgment may be inevitable. If you find yourself there, recognize you are human and remind yourself that judgment will not help in this matter. It is human to make excuses. It is also human to take action and make choices.

This exercise is about collecting information that will enable you to take action instead of being stuck in excuse inertia. Once you give energy to excuses, it doesn't take much effort to keep them going, but it can take a lot of effort to stop them and switch to action. This is where calling yourself out works, because you say the excuse aloud, call it out as bullsh*t and shift the energy. Calling out the crap helps to break the pattern.

Action time:

Take one day and journal how many times you find yourself saying, "I wish I could do this... ‹specify› but that... ‹specify›"

Notice what excuses fill in the gaps. Calling it out works like this...

> "Sure, so-and-so ‹insert name› is happy, but look what they have been given. If I had that, I could be happy too..."

Ready?

*"Cough, cough! Bullsh*t!"*

Okay, now try again.

*"I would eat better but... BULLSH*T!"*

*"I would exercise but... BULLSH*T!"*

*"I would apply for this job but... BULLSH*T!"*

Notice how many times in a day you make excuses for not doing what you want, not getting what you want, not making it to where you want to go.

Now go back to your excuses and write down three action steps you could take that would either change the outcome or move you closer to where you want to be.

Then choose one step to begin implementing now. You might be resistant at first to calling yourself out on your own BS, but when you take 'radical personal responsibility' for your happiness, you choose a life filled with happiness.

CHAPTER 18

Life Makes No Promises

For a significant period of time, I was angry at life in general. I felt gipped because my mother had passed away when I was so young. Why did most of my friends get to grow up with a mom and I didn't? The most famous of my questions: What did I do to deserve this? I carried the perception of life being unfair for many years. I found evidence of this 'truth' over and over.

This world is filled with abject horror and there is plenty of tragedy out there. However, I learned that if I wanted to be truly happy, I had to allow myself to see the good, the beautiful, the wondrous parts of life. You may be unsurprised to hear that I went through many phases where seeing the miraculous and the spectacular felt impossible, until one day I came to a profound realization. In order for me to open my eyes to beauty, I had to come to terms with the fact that life doesn't promise anything at all, other than life itself. Life makes no promises. It simply promises to be life.

If you ask someone what their definition of life is, it would probably include breathing, but further detail would be more unique and individual. If life promises to be something for one person and something different for someone else, disappointment or broken promises will be inevitable somewhere. Life can't actually make promises though. It wasn't ripping me off at all. I was angry because life didn't fit the mold that I believed it was supposed to fit and because I was hurting in a big way. How many times have we heard the line, "Life is what we make it"? It might be a cliché, but it's true.

By no means does this justify the pain, suffering, tragedy and horror in the world. Yet living a life filled with happiness meant learning to be with uncomfortable feelings sometimes. I also had to let go of the imaginary promise that life is always fair, which I desperately desired to be true. That pretend promise kept me going for years, because I believed I was going to get something in return for all this suffering and hardship. That isn't necessarily true. Why? Because happiness isn't an exchange system.

These realizations felt extremely heavy, intense and uninspiring, especially without the guarantee that I would get something amazing at the end of it all. Then one miraculous but uneventful day, I decided I simply had to let go of trying to make life fair and instead focus on making it good. Waiting for someone to repay me for the suffering or for luck to show up in exchange for my challenges was futile. Now I would put my efforts towards making life good in the way I knew how. My journey became about figuring out where to find the good, find the happy, even create the happy, instead of making life fair. Unfortunately, I was not blessed with superpowers to grant justice in life, but I can bring in more happiness. I would argue that you can too and so can everyone else.

How did I stop being angry at life?

The answer to this question doesn't lie in a specific order. Sometimes we heal or recover all at once rather than in any sequential fashion. However, I began by giving myself permission to be upset about whatever situation was causing me to be unhappy. Pretending I was fine with crappy things happening and dismissing them wasn't helpful.

People would say to me, "I am sorry your mother passed away" and I would respond, "Why? You didn't kill her?" I shudder at the thought of this now. I was trying to act tough, like I didn't need their acknowledgment or support. This pretend barrier would leave me feeling yuckier inside every time I used it. I used to say her death 'happened for a reason' to try to find some kind of justification and prevent me getting upset. Honestly, this didn't release the pain of her death either. It just felt like the thing to say. Perhaps if I said it enough, I would believe it.

I recognize the adversities in my life have helped me better understand and appreciate happiness. Would I have the same depth of understanding of happiness if they hadn't happened? Did these tragedies need to happen in order for me to grow and learn? The answer to those questions I will never know; that is not how my life has unfolded.

I would never say I am 'glad' my challenges in life have happened either, because that would be an outright lie. I am not glad my mother died; for that, I am sad. I was angry for losing special moments with my young children when I was dealing with my own cancer. I don't dismiss these events by saying they 'happened for a reason'. I would never suggest someone had to experience something for a specific reason, implying there would be no other way for them to learn a necessary lesson. Reading an article by Tim J. Lawrence called *Everything Doesn't Happen For a Reason* allowed me to bring my thoughts on my difficult experiences into perspective and release the belief that I somehow deserved to have this suffering or I wouldn't have learned.

I miss the carefree happiness that I know existed in me once a upon a time, that piece that didn't know what loss, betrayal or fear really meant. I also appreciate that a grateful kind of happiness exists in me now, because I have seen another side of life. I have learned to separate my mother's death from imagined promises of what life owed me.

Personally, I have always found peace in not feeling the need to ask the universal question of why she had to die. Somehow, I knew instinctively I would never know that answer and didn't need to know. Some questions just don't get answered, nor should they be. There lies the paradox of life. Questions unanswered can leave frustration, anger and resentment. And questions unanswered can also leave mystery, wonderment and awe.

When I embraced the idea that life makes no promises, it allowed me to free up a significant amount of space and reconnect with happy. It meant separating my individual experiences from a generalized perspective I had created about life itself. Not being angry at life doesn't mean I don't feel angry, sad or jealous. It means I direct the anger towards the specific situation but don't turn it into a blanket belief about life. I understand that this crappy thing happening does not translate into life ripping me off. I still recognize the hurt. And man, do I feel that hurt. Yet it's no longer twisted into bitter resentment.

For me, letting go of anger didn't happen when I became aware it existed. I needed a few positive internal shifts to happen before release became possible. I have a roster of things that need to be a part of my life for me feel strong enough, courageous enough and disciplined enough to do what is required to live as joyfully as possible. This is where the power of choice comes into play. These are the many sides of happy.

CHAPTER 19

Recognizing Privilege

Once, I had someone tell me I should be grateful for how privileged I am. I remember feeling angry and thinking, *Privileged? Who the hell are you calling privileged? You don't know my story.* Oh naïve me.

The 'life owes me something' attitude is a sign of a privileged perspective. People don't have to know my story to see the automatic privilege that comes along with being a white female born in Canada. I don't know what it feels like to wake up with an automatic obstacle, barrier or judgment placed upon me because of who I am: ethnicity, sexual orientation, ability and so on. Sure, gender applies to me, but it's not something I face daily.

Here's the bottom line. True happiness doesn't come at the expense of someone else's happiness. Does that mean we can't be happy until the entire world is happy? No. However, if we are in a place of privilege, using that privilege in even the smallest ways to advocate for those who can't advocate for themselves becomes an important piece of the choosing happy process; it's another side of happy. It is heavy when we think of those who are still suffering for ridiculous reasons. We can't wave a magic wand and solve all the world's issues in one fell swoop. However, we can make a small impact on a daily basis. Whether it's being mindful of what we share, who we follow on social media as well as, speaking up for those who can't.

When we stand up for acceptance, compassion, love and peace, we maintain our integrity and feed into a powerful give-back loop of choosing happy. So if I'm privileged does that give me an advantage for healing and finding happiness? In some ways, yes. In other ways, privilege can negatively impact the development of resilience therefore, negatively impacting one's ability to choose happy. Thus, are the advantages of privilege the perfect equation for happiness? Definitely not. Other work is involved.

I know some will read these previous two life lessons and think, *What a crazy woman to ever believe life should owe her anything.* And I agree. It's not just crazy but entitled. However, without learning the lesson that life does not promise anything, my ability to be happy would remain limited. Privilege does not equate to happiness it equates to privilege. Expectations do not equate to happiness. In order to embrace the deepest joys in life, it is crucial to understand that life makes no promises *and* that those born into privilege need to be aware and use that privilege to shift the dynamic for those who weren't.

When I let go of my expectations of life and learned more about my obligation to do something with the privilege I have, I freed up space to understand more truth about myself and life. I tapped into spirituality. It is difficult to digest this part of ourselves, given the often deep-rooted feelings of shame. However, this work is crucial. Working towards acceptance and equality for all brings a sense peace. And feeling internal peace is choosing happy.

The other aspect of privilege is recognizing the gift of life, of being alive today in this moment. Not everyone is afforded that privilege and how long any of us get to experience life isn't guaranteed. It's up to us to use the time we do have, in a way that is the meaningful and as positive experience creating as possible.

CHAPTER 20

Asking for Help and Finding Connection

A strong community connection is a pillar for happiness, because allowing others to help you and being willing to receive support is important during difficult times. Letting others in is important all the time, in fact. I look at the ability to receive help from others in such a different light than I used to, when I viewed myself as weak or incapable for asking. We all need support to fill us up again when we are depleted. Once we feel full and supported, we can go back to helping others in need. Helping others is itself a pillar of happiness. Therefore, when we need help, we should take it. This allows you to give back and experience the beautiful sense of choosing happy.

Sometimes in that processing or foggy phase, asking for help can seem like your own personal mountain. Take a deep breath and simply ask.

Sometimes help comes from the most unexpected places too. Part of choosing happy when facing obstacles or embracing life is being open, which is not easy in itself and takes practice. It will serve you though. With happiness and other positive traits like resiliency or confidence, there is a genetic component, a situational component and a component that can be learned. Recovering from tragic events and still being able to choose happy is absolutely possible. Research tells us it will be easier for some, but don't discount practice. It's accessible for all.

Connection can be hard for those who have endured much hurt or trauma in their lifetime. We become fearful of letting anyone in because the hurt experienced and the risk of it happening again far outweighs the upside of connecting. If you feel this way, healing that hurt and connecting to your inner worth and empowerment are the initial steps to take before jumping into connecting with 'just anyone'.

By nature, I am an optimist and I trust easily. On occasion, I have been burned pretty badly. Yet I hold fast and true with the value of loving and connecting to others. Through years of healing and understanding, I recognize that connection doesn't mean being subservient or complacent. I have boundaries and I try hard to honour them. I have learned the art of walking away when my happiness is compromised. I have let go of relationships that people told me I was obligated to maintain simply because of who that person was in my life. By letting go of that unhealthy connection, I was able to let in the good ones, where both parties' needs and mutual respect are maintained.

Connecting with Brené Brown's brilliant statement "I am worthy" made me see we are all worthy of healthy, loving, supportive relationships and connections. Therefore, we need to behave from a healthy, loving, respectful perspective and hold those standards for those we connect with. We also need to make space for the effort that connection can require and the mistakes that we will inevitably make, as well as the mistakes of those we connect with.

Go back to your definition of happiness. If your connections fuel that happy feeling, they are worth the effort and will support your choosing happy adventure.

CHAPTER 21

Celebrations

I could end *The Many Sides of Happy* on any one of thousands of little life reminders that all contribute to happiness, but where better to leave it than discussing celebration? I am a firm, firm, firm believer in celebrating! Life is hard enough at times. Stopping to celebrate overcoming hard moments can be the best fuel to inspire your efforts to keep going.

Education meant everything to my Dad. He grew up extremely poor and always wished the best for his children, as so many parents do. He believed that through education his kids could have a better life than he did. His one hard and steadfast piece of advice to me was the importance of an education. In his stern 'I'm not mad at you but you definitely need to listen' voice, he would say, "Mieka, you have to get an education whether you use it or not. It's one thing nobody can take from you. They can take your money and people can leave you, but you will always have your education. You never know when it will come in handy." He practically bled this advice. In my heart, I am so grateful for it. I got an education and will forever have gratitude for my dad pushing me to do it.

When I graduated from university, I knew it would be a shining moment for my dad. However, when I finished school, he had already suffered his heart attack and was experiencing the effects of brain damage. He didn't even remember I attended university. I was so angry at the world in that moment. And there was absolutely no way I was attending my graduation!

Once again, deep in my pity party about the unfairness of life (and saying things like: "of course this is happening to me uh-gain"), the world was robbing me of an experience that everyone else got to have. I am well aware the pettiness of my pity party. Very few people in the world get to graduate university. At the same time, it hurt. I felt gipped. I had worked hard in school, and at this milestone moment in my life, I was going to be reminded of loss yet again. Obviously, my mom wasn't going to be there. And my dad would be there in body with no mental awareness.

My sister, the incredible human being that she is, basically forced me to go. She told me there was no way I was going to miss my convocation. I was going to attend, even if she had to drag me there. I reluctantly obliged.

To my surprise, that warm summer day was lovely. I got to see my friends graduate too. My family attended and my dad beamed. I felt a sense of joy. In that moment, he knew what was happening. He wouldn't remember it a few short minutes later, but we had a special moment that I could cherish.

So caught up in my pity party previous to my graduation, I didn't even realize I'd made the Dean's list. I know it's ridiculous to be unaware of this accomplishment. I was pleasantly surprised! I was given lovely gifts and had a beautiful celebration.

I came to a potent awareness about my choices and willingness to stay a victim of my circumstances that day. It made me greatly uneasy. Had I not gone to my graduation because I felt sorry for myself, I would've missed out on so much and regretted it. I would never have known I made the Dean's list, which was such a validation for years of hard work and all-nighters. I would've missed out on that brief special moment when I looked at my dad's smile and saw that somewhere deep inside he knew. I would've missed out on the celebration, the feeling of accomplishment. Sitting in angry mode would have robbed me of an experience I cherish to this day.

Many times in my life, a part of me has found a sense of empowerment and validation from being able to play the victim role of 'poor me'. I lost my mom so young, poor me. My family dynamic growing up was extremely challenging and painful, poor me. However, when I operated in that place, opportunities for celebration, for growth, for love, for life, for happiness were passing me by.

Acknowledging and being real with what was bothering me, and at the same time not allowing it to stop me from moving forward and celebrating the awesome parts of my life, was profound. I didn't back into the shadows and give away my power to my circumstances. I acknowledge that I had and still have support. I am aware of how powerful and important that support is and was. Yet when it came down to the final analysis, the choice to celebrate or not celebrate was ultimately mine.

There is a moment when we choose. There always is.

The inertia to succumb to my feelings and retreat was strong and overwhelming. My skin crawled. My head, my heart, my bones ached in agony. However, when I leaned in and chose to go to my graduation anyway, I received an empowering experience. I witnessed the possibility that I could choose in spite of my circumstances. Nothing about my circumstances was different when I chose to go. My mom had still died many years earlier. My dad asked me if I went to university before we even got to the car. It hurt *and* I felt alive. I accomplished a massive goal and I was so glad I did.

Convocation ceremony or not, I would've graduated school. However, the act of celebration is what truly allowed my accomplishment to land. It felt amazing. That moment of recognition and receiving was extremely powerful and exceptionally positive. You see, in celebration mode, it is really difficult to be simultaneously in victim mode, slave to sh*tty circumstances.

This was a bit of dilemma at times and here's why. If I stayed in victim mode, I could blame my stupid, irrational and hurtful choices on the fact I had gone through some bad times. In order to feel the benefits and beauty of the celebrations, I couldn't be in victim mode. Coming out of victim mode meant owning the fact I had made stupid choices too. I didn't necessarily want to be accountable for some of my behavior. Even thinking of holding myself to account for some of the silly, stupid, hurtful things I had done was more than I could handle. I was at a crossroads.

Leading and living a happy life, whether I was conscious of it at the time or not, has always been what I wanted. Therefore, I knew I was going to have to accept responsibility for all aspects of my life. I needed to be accountable for what I wanted to do next. I also needed to take ownership of the mistakes and choices I wasn't proud of, the things I had been procrastinating on, even some major decisions that I knew I had to make to move forward in the future to ensure I was honouring my happy path. How was I going to get there? Talk about heavy and intimidating. Except I knew it wasn't a recipe for total devastation...

I knew if I took responsibility, if I chose to show up anyhow, that there was a possibility for celebration and unexpected surprises. The possibility for beautiful smiles, hugs and love. So many times, this has felt way too risky. Can I handle the consequences? Will I be thrown into darkness? Will I pass a point of no return? The truth is I don't know. I don't have a crystal ball that I can look into and say, "Yep, if I do this, for sure, no question about it, I will be happy." There are days I wish I did.

The only thing I knew for certain was this: if I didn't accept responsibility, I gave away my opportunity for choosing happy altogether.

So in this moment, I celebrate with you. I celebrate you opening this book. I celebrate you being courageous enough to take responsibility for your happiness. I celebrate finishing writing this book. I celebrate life itself. And I celebrate the possibility of overcoming trauma and adversity by living a life of choosing happy.

APPENDIX A

The Happy Meditation Practice (10 mins)

Take a seated position or lie down.

If you wish, diffuse essentials oils, have a pillow to sit on in a color you like or play soft music that you connect to and brings you a calming response.

Take three breaths into the depths of your belly. Feel like you are pulling in so much breath that it may even expand beyond the boundaries of your body.

Once you've taken these three breaths, take three more, just as big and broad. This time, at the end of your inhale, hold each breath for three seconds. Once you get to the end of the three seconds, allow yourself a dramatic exhale while uttering the word 'release' in your head. (This doesn't mean that you need to let go of all your troubles and worries instantaneously. How nice would that be though?!) Simply let go of any tension or distractions that it's possible for you to release in that moment. Foster that platform for release.

After you have finished that final breath, take a moment to settle in and to create a feeling of being grounded, supported and safe.

Pause in this intention and focus for the next 10 breaths. Count them and feel more rooted and firm in your space with each exhale.

Start to focus on your breath in a different way. Assigning each inhale and exhale with a task.

While inhaling think about pulling up energy from the base of the pelvis. Draw it up from the earth beneath you. That energy has a specific role. It is filled with love, support and joy.

As you continue to inhale, feel how that breath and energy fills your entire body. Give it permission to move to all corners of your body.

As you work with this inhale, you may notice areas of your body where you feel resistance or can't access. This is where the exhale comes in.

Each time you need to exhale, charge it with the role of releasing. Let go of barriers, obstacles, tension, judgments or anything else that makes sense to you, anything that gets in the way of your happiness.

Stay with this cycle of breath, observing each inhale, noticing where your body is receptive to this energy and where it isn't, observing each exhale, releasing what you can.

Be compassionate with yourself if you are unable to let go of anything during this meditation.

Give your breath and energy permission to fill you. Be receptive to the energy, support and happiness that the breath can bring.

Give *yourself* permission to let go. Release the stories that tell you you're wrong, undeserving, silly, crazy, unworthy.

Aubrey de Graf once said, "Don't cling to a mistake just because you spent a lot of time making it."

Embracing this sentiment gives you a stronger ability to let go.

Recognize what you are ready to release and be kind to yourself when you can't. With time and practice, the ability to let go of more and more will strengthen.

You may notice that you feel more spacious and open. Look at this feeling of lightness as a blank canvas. Then start to paint on that canvas. Paint anything that makes you feel safe, understood, excited and loved.

Recognize that you are filling yourself up with those sensations. The feeling of love and happiness is not based on what exists outside of you. It is a feeling you can cultivate inside.

Once your canvas appears full of beautiful meaningful images, take a moment to embrace it, welcome it, honor it and be grateful for it.

Take 10 more breaths simply sitting with your canvas. Cultivate a strong connection to it.

Once complete bow your head forward to seal your meditation and slowly open your eyes to reconnect with your environment around you.

APPENDIX B

The Happy Workout (20 mins)

I have created the following 20-minute happy workout and a 20-minute happy yoga practice that you can choose as part of your physical activity action plan. If you are new to exercise, have injuries, are pregnant, think you might be pregnant or are ill, be sure to consult with a physician before starting either of these programs.

No extra equipment is required. Just your body and a bottle of water (preferably reusable glass or stainless steel).

This workout is designed to get the blood pumping and create a feel-good response. There is an element of challenge built into this workout strategically. This helps the endorphin release. If you find yourself feeling overly challenged, take a moment to connect with the overall purpose of this workout as outlined in step one. Then instead of resisting the challenge, embrace it from the understanding that it is creating a happier you.

NOTE: Reading the exercises alone will not create the happy results. You actually have to do the exercise! This is part of the happy groundwork that requires action. You can do it. Start now!

Exercise	Description	Image
Step one: *Intention*	When starting your workout, take a moment to close your eyes and connect with an intention. Say the affirmation "I am happy" or an affirmation you connect with that supports your happiness. Pause here with it for up to a minute, inhaling and exhaling, creating a connection.	
Step two: *Stairs*	Near where you intend to work out, find a set of stairs. Start at the bottom and climb to the top, stepping two stairs at a time. (You can use the railing for balance but try not to lean on it.) Skip every other step and be sure to watch your footing. Push off with the entire foot of the lead leg, squeezing your glutes as you transition to the next step. Each time you take a new step, use the same leg to step with. At the top of the stairs, turn around and go back down one step at a time. Do not skip any steps. Repeat the entire flight of stairs (or approximately 15 to 20 steps) on the same leg three to five times. Switch legs and repeat the sequence.	

Step two (variation): **Lunges**	If you live or work out in a space without stairs, you can do stationary lunges. Start with either leg. Take a large step forward, landing on the entire foot of the lead leg. Bend both knees, making sure the knee of the lead leg is directly over the top of the ankle, not past it. Ensure the center of the knee is in line with the second toe, not collapsing inward or outward. Stack the upper body so the shoulders are directly over the top of the hips, hold the belly in tight and bend the back knee deep enough to approximately 6 to 10 inches above the floor, allowing the front knee to come to a 90-degree angle . Repeat this 20 times, then change lead legs. When transitioning back to an upright position, push off the heel of the lead leg, pull the abs in tight and squeeze the glutes, allowing the lead leg to return to a full standing position beside the other leg.	

Step three: **Plank**	This exercise is phenomenal, versatile and extremely functional. It's important to recognize it will take time to build up strength and endurance with this exercise so be patient. Be more concerned with your form over the length of time you are holding it. In the beginning, plank can be done in shorter intervals, eventually extending the length of time you hold it. You can choose to do the plank either on your elbows or your hands, on your knees or on your toes with the legs extended. Lying in a prone position (belly down) bring your elbows or hands directly beneath your shoulders. Keeping them shoulder distance apart, lift your chest so the upper body is elevated above the hands/elbows. (You want to feel like your elbows or hands are pulling towards one another, like they are trying to touch one another but never will. This helps stabilize the shoulders as well as engage the core.) Lift the hips in a straight line with the shoulders, knees down or on your tiptoes. Either way, there should be a long line from your head to your knees or your toes.	

	Tighten your belly by engaging the core feeling like you are pulling the belly button back towards your spine. Squeeze your inner thighs towards one another; this action is known as thigh adduction and behaves as a switch for the nervous system to get the abdominal muscles firing. That's what you want!	
Step four: *Back Extensions*	Lying prone (belly down), bring the legs together so the inner thighs touch and the tops of the feet are firmly against the ground or mat. Flex the quads, hamstrings and glutes, so the front of the thigh, back of the thigh and bum feel firm or the muscles feel like they're firing. Engage the core by imagining you are pulling the belly button back towards the spine. Line your up arms along the side of the body with the palms of the hands facing inward. In the photo arms are shown overhead but this is a more advanced way of doing the exercise. If arms overhead is feeling ok feel free to do the exercise that way otherwise, have arms at sides reaching back. You also do not have to lift the upper body up as high, as is shown in the image. Draw the chin in slightly so the back of the neck is lengthened, and the top of the head is reaching forward.	

Back extensions con't.	Draw the shoulder blades towards one another to fire up the back body, then begin to lift and lower the shoulders through a comfortable range of motion working the muscles of the lower back. Should you experience pinching or sharp pain of any sort, discontinue this exercise.	
Step five: Wall Sit	Place your back against a wall and then step your feet approximately 18 to 24 inches away. The distance will vary depending on how long your legs are. Slide your back down the wall so that your legs make a 90-degree angle. The knees should be directly over the top of the ankles, not past them, as that can create too much pressure on the knee joint. If there is any pain in the knee don't bend as deep. Distribute your weight evenly throughout each foot, being aware not to push your body weight in to the balls of your feet. While leaning against the wall, feel as if you are trying to squeeze the inner thighs towards one another and pull your belly button back towards your spine to engage the core.	

wall sit con't	Should you feel any pain or discomfort in the knees during this exercise, either lift the hips slightly higher up the wall, increasing the angle at the knees, or discontinue this exercise. For an extra challenge, take your arms above your head, with or without weights, be careful not to arch in the lower back.	
Step six: Knee-Ups	Standing tall and engaging the core (pulling the belly button back towards the spine), hold your hands out in front of you at shoulder height. While balancing on one leg, lift the opposite knee and raise it as high as you can get it, aiming to tap your outstretched hand. Alternate from left to right. To increase the intensity, you can jump to switch the knees. Alternatively, keep it low impact, lifting the opposite leg, always leaving one foot firmly on the ground.	

Full Circuit Repetitions

For the purpose of endorphin release, complete the circuit in sequential order to create a cardiovascular effect.

Use a timer and spend one minute doing the stairs exercise on each leg, then one minute of each of the following exercises back-to-back taking a minute recovery break between each full circuit. It may take time to work up to doing each exercise for one full minute, so take breaks as you need, but don't give up! And remember consistency is key.

This is one of the thousands of workouts or exercises you could choose to do to create a happy-hormone-producing experience. The Canadian Physical Activity Guidelines recommend a minimum of 150 minutes of moderate to vigorous aerobic physical activity a week in bouts of 10 minutes or more to achieve maximum health benefits. Adding in muscle- and bone-strengthening activities twice a week is extremely beneficial.

APPENDIX C

The Happy Yoga Practice (20 mins)

I highly recommend having your favourite playlist on in the background and fully encourage intermittent dancing and singing breaks!

This practice is designed to get your heart rate up gently, while creating the mindful connection to an affirmation. Choose an affirmation that resonates with you and is positive in nature. It could be "I am grateful for all the blessings in my life," "I am connecting to joy" or any other positive affirmation that resonates with you.

Exercise	Description	Image
Corpse Pose (Svanasana)	Lying on your back take three deep breaths. Allow the breath to soften and take a moment to reflect on the affirmation you want to use for this practice. Repeat it three times.	

Supine Twist (Jathara Parivritti)	Transition onto your back, draw your right knee into your chest and wrap a strap or towel around the base of the foot, holding both ends in your left hand. Extend the right leg, the knee doesn't need to extend fully, so respect your body's limits. Extend the right arm out and anchor it down engaging the core. Bring the right leg to come across the body, allowing the spine to gently twist. Do not force the leg to touch the floor as the leg does not need to touch the floor. for a lying supine twist. Turn your head in the opposite direction, if comfortable. Hold for five breaths. Repeat on the opposite side.	
Table (Bharmanasana)	Roll all the way onto your right side and then press yourself up into a table-top position on your hands and knees, where your knees are directly beneath your hips and your hands are directly beneath your shoulders. Feel as if you are trying to drag your hands towards you knees and your knees towards your hands firing up the core. Hold this engagement in the body for three breaths.	

Table with increased core engagement. (Bharmanasana)	Tuck your toes under and lift your knees so they hover an inch off the floor. Feel as if you are dragging the hands towards the feet and the feet towards the hands. Hold this for a full five breaths. Lower your knees and repeat twice more, each time holding for five breaths.	
Downward Dog (Adho Mukha Svanasana)	Once complete, press your hips up towards the ceiling or sky and pause in downward-facing dog. Being mindful of the shoulders, allowing them to soften so they are not tense and scrunching up towards the ears, arms are strong and not locked, fingers are spread wide and strong. Knees can be bent in this pose if needed. Take the opportunity to repeat the affirmation you stated at the beginning of your practice, this time in your mind. Pause here for five breaths.	

Plank (Uttihita Chaturanga Dandasana)	On your next inhale, shift your body into a plank pose, with knees up or down. Pause for three breaths, then press back into downward dog. Repeat plank to downward dog five more times, being sure to pause in both the plank and the downward dog poses for five breaths each.	
SEQUENCE	The following highlighted poses are structured to be done in a sequential flowing fashion.	
Mountain Pose (Tadasana)	Walk your hands to your feet, engage your core and come up to standing position. With your arms at your sides in tadasana (mountain pose) close your eyes and take three breaths connecting to your affirmation.	
Arms overhead	As you inhale, reach your arms overhead.	
Forward Fold (Uttanasana)	Exhale into a forward fold.	

Lengthen Spine/ Halfway Lift	Inhale to lengthen your spine.	
Plank Pose (Uttihita Chaturanga Dandasana)	Exhale to step back into a plank pose, knees down if you wish. Hold for three breaths.	
Lengthen Spine/Halfway Lift	walk your hands back to your feet. Inhale to lengthen your spine into a flat back (or as flat as possible).	
Forward Fold (Uttanasana)	Exhale to forward fold.	
Mountain Pose (Tadasana)	Inhale to come into a standing position.	
	Repeat the sequence above twice more.	

Chair Pose (Utkatasana)	On your next inhale reach your arms overhead, bend your knees and sit hips your back. Squeeze your inner thighs and be sure sit back so your knees do not go past your toes. Contract your abs so you don't collapse into your lower back. Pause here holding for five breaths and then begin small pulses lifting the thighs only one inch and then lowering again. Repeat this 10-times.	
Mountain Pose (Tadasana)	Come up to standing position. With your arms at your sides in tadasana (mountain pose) close your eyes and take three breaths connecting to your affirmation.	
Arms overhead	As you inhale, reach your arms overhead	
Forward Fold (Uttanasana)	Exhale into a forward fold.	

Halfway Lift/ Lengthen Spine	Inhale to lengthen your spine	
Plank Pose (Uttihita Chaturanga Dandasana)	Exhale walking your hands out into to step a plank pose, knees down if you wish. Hold for three breaths	
Side Plank (Vasisthasana)	Shifting onto your right hand, making sure it is directly beneath your shoulder, or your right elbow if your wrists are sensitive, come onto your right knee with your left leg extended for side plank. If you would like more of a challenge, come onto the outside of your right foot with the left foot on top. Hold this pose for five to ten breaths and then switch to the left side.	
Plank (Uttihita Chaturanga Dandasana)	Come back into plank and hold for one breath. Then walk your hands back to your feet.	

Halfway Lift/Lengthen Spine	Inhale to lengthen your spine.	
Forward Fold (Uttanasana)	Exhale to forward fold.	
Mountain Pose (Tadasana)	Inhale to come to a standing position.	
Standing with hands interlaced behind your back.	Exhale and interlace your hands behind your back. If this is too much for your shoulders, grab onto a towel with both hands behind you, elbows extended. Hold for five breaths letting the tension in the shoulders melt away. Again, pause to connect with your affirmation.	

Tree Pose (Vrksasana)	As you exhale, release your hands, anchor down into the right foot, engage your core and prepare to lift the left foot into tree pose. For some, resting the right tiptoes gently on the floor may be easier, or you can place your foot above or below your left knee, with the right knee turned out to the side. Hands can be at heart center or arms extended overhead. Pause here for five breaths, repeating your affirmation. Switch to the other side and repeat, holding for five breaths.	
Mountain Pose (Tadasana)	Pause to plant both feet into mountain pose, repeating your affirmation.	
Arms overhead	Inhale to reach your arms overhead.	
Forward Fold (Uttanasana)	Exhale to forward fold.	

Half Way Lift/ Lengthen Spine	Inhale hands to your shins and flatten out the back.	
Forward Fold (Uttanasana)	Exhale to forward fold.	
Plank (Uttihita Chaturanga Dandasana)	Step back into a plank position, knees up or down. Pause here for three breaths and then do three to five push-ups, knees up or down. Once you've completed the last push-up, lower your body down to rest on your belly. Pause here with your head resting on your hands for five breaths, connecting with your affirmation.	
Sphynx Pose (Salamba Bhujangasana)	As you inhale, bring the elbows beneath your shoulders and lift your chest into sphynx pose. Legs are extended behind you with the core engaged. Feet and knees are together. Respect your back here. Do not force yourself into this position if you feel any pinching in the lower back. Hold for five breaths.	

Modified Locust Pose (Salabhasana)	Lower onto your belly and extend your arms at your sides with the palms facing down and the thumbs away from your body. Plant the shoulder blades onto your back, opening across the chest. Engage the core, keep the legs together and firm, then lift the chest with your hands reaching behind here. Hold for five breaths. Repeat three times. To increase intensity an option is to reach arms overhead with shoulders planted firmly on the back body, relaxed away from the ears.	
Childs Pose (Balasana)	As you exhale, press back into child pose and hold here for five breaths. Connect once again with the original affirmation. Maybe sing or wiggle to your playlist of choice. Pause to smile, pause to breathe, pause to think of three things you are grateful for.	

Seated Forward Fold (Paschimottanasana)	Shift your legs out from underneath you and come into a seated position with your legs extended long in front of you. If this hurts your back, sit up on a block, pillow or blanket. You can use a strap, towel or tie here if you know your hamstrings are tight. When you're ready, using either your strap to wrap around the soles of the feet or your index and middle fingers, grab on to the big toes. Inhale to lengthen the spine and exhale to fold forward. Take 10 complete breaths here. Give your body permission to let go of tension, stress, to-do lists, anger, or whatever you think would be helpful. Simply allow yourself to feel less tension.	

Gentle Seated Twist (Ardha Matsyendrasana)	On your next inhale, bend your left leg and cross your right foot over your left leg so the soul of your right foot lands on the floor. Reach the right hand behind you on the floor with either a flat palm or on the tips of the fingers. Bend the opposite left elbow hook it over the right knee or wrap the opposite arm around the right leg and hug the leg into your body. If this is too much sit cross legged or up on a block and take your right hand behind you to support, you and the back of your left palm to the outside of your right knee. Inhale to lengthen your spine. Exhale to engage the core and come into a gentle twist. Take this time to let go of anything that you feel you can, using that twist to make space in your body. Hold this for five to ten breaths and then switch to the opposite side.	

Butterfly Pose (Baddhakonasana)	Shift your legs so the soles of your feet come together, and your knees fall to your sides. Blocks or blankets beneath your knees can be helpful here if you feel any pinching or pulling. If the inner thighs and hips are tight, take your hands behind you to support you. If it feels okay, take your hands to the outside of your feet and move into a forward fold. Take three deep sighs here. Be dramatic and use that effort to create an internal release. Stay here for another five to ten breaths.	
Corpse Pose (Svanasana)	Once complete, come onto your back into savasana for your final resting pose. Pause here, reconnecting with your affirmation, then take the opportunity to settle into the mat or towel beneath you and let yourself feel good. Stay here for a minimum of five minutes, longer if you can.	

Easy Seated Pose with Hands at Heart Center. (Sukhasana with Namaste Hands)	Once complete, roll onto your side and press yourself up into a seated position. Bring your hands to heart center. Take a moment to repeat your affirmation and then bow your head to and say "Namaste" to complete your practice.	

APPENDIX D

Root Chakra Yoga Practice

Affirmations:

"I am safe"

"I am supported"

"I am strong"

"I am ready"

Exercise	Description	Image
Mountain Pose (Tadasana)	Begin in tadasana (mountain pose). Stand tall, rooting down through (preferably bare) feet. This is even more beneficial if you can do it in nature. Pause, holding your hands at your sides, palms facing forward. Stand here for five long complete breaths. Repeat an affirmation focused on safety, stability and strength, accessing the abundance of life or receiving the joy and happiness that life has to offer.	

Arms Overhead	Inhale, keeping the core engaged reach your arms overhead.	
Forward Fold (Uttanasana)	Exhale, drawing the belly back to forward fold. Knees can be bent here if feeling too much tension.	
Lengthen Spine/ Halfway lift	Inhale to lengthen halfway lift body with hands to shins. Core is engaged.	
Plank or Table (Uttihita Chaturanga Dandasana)	Exhale to step back to into plank or table pose. Hands are directly beneath the shoulders, squeeze the inner thighs towards one another and draw the belly back, being careful not to dump into the low back. Hold plank or table pose for five to ten breaths. Feeling the support of the earth beneath you, breathe into the strength and stability of your body. Be as still as you can, envisioning a strong foundation built from your new beliefs of the love and support life has to offer.	

Downward Facing Dog (Adho Mukha Svanasana)	Once the five to ten breaths are complete, exhale to press back into downward-facing dog. Hips pressing high towards the ceiling, drawing the heals towards the ground, if feeling too much tension bend the knees. Press the weight of the body towards the back of the mat, feel the sensation of the hands dragging towards the back of the mat to engage the lats (back muscles) and release tension in the shoulders. The core is tight. Feel the stability of the ground beneath your hands and feet. Feel supported and safe. Hold downward-facing dog for five full breaths. With each exhale, make the conscious decision to let go of even a portion of those beliefs that no longer serve you or your decision for choosing happy.	
Lengthen Spine/Halfway Lift	When the fifth breath is complete, step forward to your hands. Inhale to lengthen your spine.	
Forward Fold (Uttanasana)	Exhale to forward fold.	
Arms Overhead	Inhale, reaching your arms overhead. Exhale to bring your hands to heart center.	

Mountain Pose (Tadasana)	Pause in mountain pose for another five breaths, grounding down through the feet, feeling strong, stable and supported.	
Arms Overhead	Inhale, reaching your arms overhead.	
Forward Fold (Uttanasana)	Exhale to forward fold.	
Lengthen Spine/Halfway Lift	Inhale to lengthen.	
Plank (Uttihita Chaturanga Dandasana)	Exhale and step back into plank pose.	

Adho Mukha Svanasana (Downward Facing Dog)	Press back into downward-facing dog.	
Low Lunge with Optional Crescent Lunge (Anjaneyasana)	Step the right leg forward and place the back-left knee down. Fold the mat over if there is too much pressure beneath your knee. Feel like you are trying to drag the back-left knee forward and the front right foot back, firing up the hamstrings on the right leg. Pause with the hands on either side of the foot for two full breaths, connecting with the sensation of feeling grounded, safe and strong. On the next inhale, reach your arms overhead. If possible, lift up the back-left knee. Pause here, holding crescent warrior pose, feeling strong, stable, capable of creating a new foundation supporting you in your choosing happy journey.	
Downward Dog (Adho Mukha Svanasana)	Place both hands back on the ground and step the left foot back to meet the right in and press back into Downward Facing Dog.	
Low Lunge Optional Crescent Warrior Opposite Foot Forward (Anjaneyasana)	Switch to the opposite leg, stepping the left leg forward releasing your back right knee down.	
	Repeat the highlighted lunging sequence three times	

Mountain Pose (Tadasana)	Pause in mountain pose and repeat the affirmation either aloud or in your head. "Life supports me through all my challenges and growth. I love life."	
Seated forward fold (Paschimottanasana)	Transition to a seated position, extending your legs in front of you. Sit up on a block or blanket if you back or hip flexors are aggravated. Inhale to lengthen the spine and exhale to forward fold reaching hands towards the knees, shins or toes depending on hamstring flexibility. Hold for five breaths repeating the affirmation, "Life supports me through all my challenges and growth. I love life."	
Corpse Pose (Svanasana)	Transition to lying on your back palms facing up, legs relaxed, a rolled-up towel or blocks beneath your knees or head, if neck or low back is bothering you. Hold here for 5 minutes.	

APPENDIX E

Sacral Chakra Yoga Practice

Affirmations:

"I take the time to enjoy all the beauty and pleasure that life has to offer"

"Laughter and joy are a priority each and every day"

"I am deserving of joy, pleasure and ease"

Exercise/Pose	Description	Image
Corpse Pose *(Svanasana)*	Start lying on your back. Stay here for five breaths focusing on unraveling any surface tension you can. Give yourself permission to let go of the burden of that tension.	

Happy baby pose (Ananda Balasana)	Thread the arms inside your legs and grab the outside edge of the feet with your hands. With the head and upper body fixed to the floor, draw your knees towards the floor, keeping your shins perpendicular. Lengthen the tailbone towards the floor. Pause here for five breaths connecting with the affirmation, "I am deserving and worthy of all the pleasures, gifts and joy that life has to offer."	
Pigeon Pose (Kapotasana)	Transition to hands and knees and bring right knee to the right wrist. Cross the right leg in front of the body, point the right toes so they are in-line with the shin. The right hip can be on the mat, on a block or a blanket if support is needed. If the back leg is bent be sure to be resting on the right hip. The back leg can also be straight. If the back leg is straight work to draw the left hip forward to square off the hips. Hold for five breaths and repeat the affirmation "I am deserving and worthy of all the pleasures, gifts and joy that life has to offer." Repeat this on the opposite side.	

Seated Angle (Upavishta Konasana)	In a seated position separate your legs into a comfortable position, if this feels too intense, an option is to sit up on a blanket or towel. Roll the shoulders down and back and reach your right hand to touch the shin or toes. Anchor down the left hip and side bend the body towards your right side. Watch the left shoulder doesn't creep to left ear, open the left side of the body away from the floor. Hold for five breaths and repeat on the opposite side.	
Downward-Facing Dog (Adho Mukha Svanasana)	Roll onto your right side, press into a seated position and then move into downward-facing dog.	
Lizard Pose (Utthan Pristhasana)	Step the right leg forward to come into a low lunge. With the left knee on the floor, option is to roll the mat up or place a towel beneath the knee to cushion if feeling discomfort. Take both hands to the inside of the right foot, come into lizard pose. You can be on your hands or your elbows. Elbows can also be on blocks. Depending on your flexibility, you can lift the back knee. Hold for five breaths. Repeat on the opposite side.	

Easy Seated Position with Optional Hands at Heart Center. (Sukhasana with Namaste Hands)	Come into a seated position option with hands at heart center repeating five times, "I am healing by recognizing I am enough and receive the love and joy life has to offer."	
Corpse Pose (Svanasana)	Transition to lying on your back palms facing up, legs relaxed, a rolled-up towel or blocks beneath your knees or head if neck or low back is bothering you. Hold here for 5 minutes.	

APPENDIX F

Solar Plexus Yoga Practice

Start seated on your mat. Close your eyes and take a deep breath. Repeat any of the above solar plexus affirmations mentioned in the Solar Plexus Section:

"I am worthy of health, love and happiness."

"I choose a life that is best for me and who I know I am."

"I am connected to my personal power and make choices for the good of myself and others."

or choose to create one that resonates with you more.

Exercise/Pose	Description	Image
Supine Twist (Jathara Parivritti)	Transition onto your back, draw your right knee into your chest and wrap a strap or towel around the base of the foot, holding both ends in your left hand. Extend the right leg, the knee doesn't need to extend fully, so respect your body's limits. Extend the right arm out and anchor it down engaging the core. Bring the right leg to come across the body, allowing the spine to gently twist. Do not force the leg to touch the floor as the leg does not need to touch the floor for a lying supine twist. Turn your head in the opposite direction, if comfortable. Hold for five breaths. Repeat on the opposite side.	

Core Single Leg Lifts	On your back. Push your hands and arms into the mat beneath you, pulling your rib cage back. Lower the right leg, bend your left knee or for a greater challenge extend your left leg towards the ceiling. Hold here for five breaths. Draw the right leg up into either a bent knee or extended position, lowering your left leg and keeping the right leg with the knee bent or extended towards the ceiling. Hold for five breaths. Be cautious not to arch the lower back. Repeat five times each on both sides in total. Draw both knees into the chest for a three-breath rest.	
Core Double Leg Lifts	Extend both legs up to the ceiling. Engage the core, being careful not to arch the lower back. Lower both legs together to hover above the ground for a count of 10. Then take a count of 10 to lift both legs back up. If this is too much on the hip flexors or back, bend your knees. Or go back to single leg lifts. Repeat three times.	

Plank Pose (Uttihita Chaturanga Dandasana)	Roll onto your belly and press up into plank pose, holding for a count of 15. Knees and/or elbows can be down if you need a modification. Repeat three times.	
Downward-Facing Dog (Adho Mukha Svanasana)	Press back to downward-facing dog and hold for five breaths.	
Mountain Pose (Tadasana)	Walk up to the top of your mat to transition to tadasana (mountain pose). Standing in tadasana, take three full breaths. Then move through three sun salutations to get the blood and energy flowing	
	Sun Salutations are Highlighted	
Mountain Pose (Tadasana)	Inhale to hold mountain pose (description above)	
Standing forward fold (Uttanasana)	Exhale to forward fold (description above)	

Lengthen Spine/ Halfway Lift	Inhale to lengthen (Description above)	
Plank (Uttihita Chaturanga Dandasana)	Exhale into plank (description above)	
Chaturanga.	Inhale to stay then bend the elbows tight at your sides. Ensuring the shoulders are over the hands and as you bend you don't drop the shoulders below a 90-degree angle. Bending the knees can be really helpful in this pose. If you are struggling with shoulder issues skip this pose and bend your knees or wiggle the knees back to eventually make your way onto your belly.	
Upward Facing Dog or Cobra (Urdhva Mukha Svanasana)	With the core engaged lift the shoulders and heart by extending the elbows and feeling a sensation of lifting the chest up and out. Gently draw the shoulders down and back onto the back body. Tops of the feet are on the floor. Hips are down for Cobra pose or hips lifted is upward dog. Core tight and legs are engaged.	

Downward-Facing Dog (Adho Mukha Svanasana)	Exhale, downward-facing dog. Hold for five breaths.	
Mountain Pose (Tadasana)	Walk back to the front of your mat and inhale to tadasana.	
Chair pose (Utkatasana)	On your next inhale reach your arms overhead, bend your knees and sit your hips back. Squeeze your inner thighs and be sure sit back so your knees do not go past your toes. Contract your abs so you don't collapse into your lower back.	

Revolved powerful pose (Revolved Utkatasana)	Exhale and begin to twist from the navel, taking your left elbow to either the inside or the outside of your right knee into revolved utkatasana (powerful pose). Watch that the left knee doesn't slide ahead of the right. Work to draw the left hip back as you twist. Hold for five full breaths repeating your chosen solar plexus affirmation. Stay in powerful pose and switch to the opposite side, taking the right elbow to the inside or outside of the left knee. This time watching for the right knee to stay in-line with the left and not slide ahead. Hold for five more breaths. Inhale back to standing. Repeat powerful pose of both sides three times.	
	Repeat One More Of the Above Highlighted Sun Salutation Repeating Your Affirmation	
Mountain Pose (Tadasana)	Inhale to Stand (See Description above)	

Standing forward fold (Uttanasana)	Exhale to Forward Fold (See Description above)	
Lengthen Spine/ Halfway Lift	Inhale to halfway lift and lengthen spine (See Description above)	
Plank (Uttihita Chaturanga Dandasana)	Exhale to step back into plank, optional knees down (See Description above)	
Chaturanga	Inhale to pause exhale to lower down or skip this pose if too hard on back or shoulders. (See Description above)	
Upward Facing Dog or Cobra (Urdhva Mukha Svanasana)	Inhale to extend arms and lift the chest, option is sphynx pose if too much on back. (See Description above)	
Downward-Facing Dog (Adho Mukha Svanasana)	Exhale press back to Downward dog. (See Description above)	

Gentle Seated Twist (Ardha Matsyendrasana)	Come into a seated position. On your next inhale, bend your left leg and cross your right foot over your left leg so the soul of your foot lands on the floor. Reach the right hand behind you on the floor with either a flat palm or on the tips of the fingers. Bend the opposite left elbow hook it over the right knee or wrap the opposite arm around the right leg and hug the leg into your body. If this is too much sit cross legged or up on a block and take your right hand behind you to support, you and the back of your left palm to the outside of your right knee. Inhale to lengthen your spine. Exhale to engage the core and come into a gentle twist. Take this time to let go of anything that you feel you can, using that twist to make space in your body. Hold this for five to ten breaths and then switch to the opposite side.	
Corpse Pose (Svanasana)	Transition onto your back for savasana for five minutes. (See Description above)	

APPENDIX G

Heart Chakra Practice

Heart Chakra Affirmations:

"I honor myself and others. I choose love."

"I choose to connect with and feed the joy that resides within."

"I am filled with love, joy and peace."

"I release the hurt that holds me back and make space for love, happiness and peace."

Exercise/Pose	Description	Image
Prone Corpse Pose (face down lying on stomach) (Svanasana)	Start by lying on your belly taking a couple of deep breaths. Repeat either out loud or in your head one of the heart chakra affirmations mentioned above. As always, if none of these particular affirmations resonates, choose one that makes sense to you around the theme of love, peace, joy or connection.	

Sphynx Pose (Salamba Bhujangasana)	Inhale and lift your shoulders into sphinx pose. Relax the glutes, draw the shoulder blades towards one another to make space across the collar bone and engage the core. Hold for five breaths focusing on the exhale to release tension across the front body.	
Childs Pose (Balasana)	Exhale to lower down and press back into childs pose. Separate the knees and have the toes touching. Reach the arms out in front and create little teepees with the hands. If this bothers your knees place a rolled-up towel between the back of the thighs and the calves. You can also kneel on a towel for extra cushion. If you have access to blocks you can place them below the forearms. Allow the heart to settle down towards the earth. Breathe space into the front of the body.	
Kneeling Pose (Vajrasana)	Walk the hands back to bring the upper body into an upright position, sitting on the heels. If this is uncomfortable, sit on a block or two still in a kneeling position. Take the arms behind you and grab opposite elbows with your hands. If your shoulders are open enough, the hands can come into reverse prayer. Hold here for five breaths, creating an open space across the heart, connecting with the intention of receiving love and compassion.	

Cat Pose (Marjaryasana)	Inhale to release the hands down and come onto all fours Exhale pressing into the hands and round the spine. Pulling the belly button and rib cage back. Spreading the shoulder blades to create more space in the back body.	
Cow Pose (Bitilasana)	Inhale to release the belly down, feeling a sensation of lifting and spreading across the chest. Core is still somewhat engaged here.	
	Alternate between inhaling into Cat pose and exhaling into Cow 3 more times.	
Downward-Facing Dog (Adho Mukha Svanasana)	Press back into downward-facing dog.	
Mountain Pose (Tadasana)	Walk your feet to your hands. Inhale into tadasana. Exhale and bring the hands to heart center reconnecting with a heart chakra affirmation.	

Standing Gentle Back Bend	Anchor into the feet. Draw the belly back to create a stable front body that will support the lower back. Either place hands with the fingertips facing down like you are sliding your hands into your back pockets, hold a strap between the hands or interlace the fingers. Inhale to lift the heart, exhale gently shift the hips forward and begin to lift the chest up and back into a gentle back bend. Be careful to listen to your body here and if it feels like too much come back into a neutral standing position. Hold for two breaths.	
Mountain Pose (Tadasana)	Exhale to engage the core, inhale to come back into tadasana.	

Standing forward fold with optional hands clasped behind the back (Uttanasana)	If possible forward fold with the hands still interlaced behind the back either using a strap or with finger tips. Keep the core engaged. Hold for 5 breaths.	
Cobra Pose **Optional Sphynx pose** (Bhujangasana)	Release the hands to the floor. Step the legs back and lower down onto the belly. Take your hands beneath your shoulders and press up into cobra pose. Unlike the picture it is not necessary to collapse in the back of the neck. Lift the heart and engage the core so as not to dump into the low back. If going on the hands is too deep of a back bend, Sphynx Pose from the elbows is an option. Hold for five breaths here.	
Locust Pose Optional Cobra or Sphynx pose (Salabhasana)	Lower down. Inhale and interlace the fingers behind the back. Lift the chest and the legs at the same time coming into locust pose. Hands can be interlaced, or you can hold onto to a towel or strap. Hold for five breaths. Repeat three times. If this bothers your back, repeat Cobra or Sphinx pose instead.	

Corpse Pose (Svanasana)	Roll over onto your back. Relax the legs and shoulders. Place a rolled-up towel beneath the neck if there is tension there or beneath the knees if there is any tension in the low back. Pause here resting for five minutes, connecting to the rhythm of love, giving and receiving.	

APPENDIX H

Throat Chakra Practice

Throat Chakra Affirmations:

"I communicate my feelings easily from a place of honesty and integrity."

"I am willing to listen with a sense of openness."

"I create opportunities to connect with my creativity and to express it."

Exercise/Pose	Description	Image
Easy Seated Pose (Sukhasana)	Start in a comfortable seated position with the legs crossed. If this is hard on the back or hips sit up on a block or pillow. Hands resting easily in your lap. Take a moment to say out loud one of the throat chakra affirmations provided above or invent an affirmation that resonates for you.	

Easy Seated Pose Bowing Head (Sukhasana)	Bow your head forward, tucking your chin and closing your eyes. Take five deep breaths here, being mindful of any light-headedness, as this type of breathwork does create some restriction in the throat area. Lift the head and allow the breath to return to its natural rhythm.	
Easy Seated Pose gentle neck rolls. (Sukhasana)	Still seated, bow your head forward and then gently roll the head to one side, continuing in a clockwise circular motion, being careful not to collapse in the back of the neck, stopping anywhere you feel tension and breathing into the tension to create an opportunity for release. Repeat this same motion in a counter-clockwise direction. Do five clockwise and five counter-clockwise movements. Return your head back to a neutral position and pause for three breaths, repeating your chosen affirmation.	

Easy Seated Pose **With Shoulder Shrugs and Lions Breath.** (Sukhasana)	Still seated, draw your shoulders up towards your ears and hold. Contract the trapezius muscles for 10 seconds, allowing the tension to build without creating pain. Then let go by sticking out your tongue and dramatically exhaling releasing any tension in the shoulders you can. Repeat this exercise three times. Pause with the shoulders relaxed and the head in a neutral position. Repeat your affirmation out loud three times.	
Corpse Pose (Svanasana)	Transition to lie down onto your back. Relax the head, neck, shoulders and legs. Place a towel beneath the knees or back of the head if experiencing any low back pain or neck pain.	

APPENDIX I

Brow Chakra Meditation

Instead of a yoga practice, this brow chakra meditation is a potent tool for accessing all the chakras. Meditation is one of the primary access activities for connecting and healing the brow chakra specifically, since using a meditation with visualization techniques helps to strengthen this chakra.

Close your eyes and take three deep breaths to calm and settle into the body.

Starting at the top of your head see if you can soften any tension you feel on the scalp, across the forehead, behind your eyes or in the jaw. Take a few breaths here and let it go. Use the breath and allow yourself to relax. As you inhale, visualize the breath creating space and clarity in your mind. Then on the next inhale think of the affirmation "I deserve to be happy; I am choosing happy." Pause with this for a moment.

Shift your focus to your throat and shoulders. See if you can let go of any effort here again, using 10 to 15 breaths to really let go. Then as you inhale, see if you can feel more space and freedom in this area. Again, repeat the affirmation quietly to yourself "I deserve to be happy; I am choosing happy."

Move your awareness to your chest and upper back. Take really deep breaths here. With each exhale, let go of heaviness or intensity that may be lingering here. Do this for 10 to 15 breaths. Then on your next inhale see if you can take that breath with a sense of lightness and ease. Once again, repeat "I deserve to be happy; I am choosing happy."

Now focus on the belly and low back. Breathe deeply here allowing the belly and the back to expand. No effort to hold anything in. Simply offer your body the possibility of release. Again take 10 to 15 breaths here. Now inhale ease and softness into both the back and the belly. Pause with your focus on the low back and belly stating the affirmation "I deserve to be happy; I am choosing happy."

Finally, bring your attention to your glutes, legs and feet. Breathe into the glutes, the front of your thighs, back of your thighs, your knees, your ankles your feet. Feel the breath travel up the front and back of your legs, letting go of any effort and muscular tension. Do this for 10 to 15 breaths. Once complete, use the breath to feel a sense of space in the joints and relaxation in the muscles. Stay with this sensation for a while. Then state "I deserve to be happy; I am choosing happy."

Now take your awareness across the entire body. Inhaling and exhaling without resistance and allowing the breath to travel effortlessly throughout.

APPENDIX J

Crown Chakra Meditation

Meditation has a powerful connection to the seventh chakra, so this brief meditation can be practiced when working to access this chakra.

Take three deep cleansing breaths. Lying on your back, draw the shoulders up to your ears, tensing and holding for three to five seconds and then letting go.

Make fists with the hands, tensing and holding for three to five seconds and then letting go.

Tense the belly tight, pulling it in and holding for three to five seconds and then letting go.

Squeeze the glutes, holding tight for three to five seconds and then letting go.

Squeeze the thighs, holding tight for three to five seconds and then letting go.

Flex the calves, holding tight for three to five seconds and then letting go.

Flex the feet, scrunching the toes and holding tight for three to five seconds and then letting go.

Repeat this one more time.

Once completed, pause and focus on the breath and the intention of connecting deeper within to 'the real you'. Stay watching the breath moving in and out of the body. Your thoughts will wander, which is normal. When you become aware of this, take a moment to acknowledge the thought and then let it drift away, bringing your awareness back to your breath.

Stay watching your breath and focus on building a place for connection to yourself, your thoughts, your feelings, dreams, wishes, hurts and frustrations. Watch as they wave in and out.

Sometimes asking a question and waiting to see how you feel or how your body reacts to the question can give way to the answers you're seeking. Doing this could reveal another question that you may need to ask before you can come to an authentic conclusion.

Spend time in that quiet place asking questions and pausing to be with the breath. As simple as it seems, this is a deep way to cultivate connection within.

References

Naseribafrouei, A., Hestad, K., Avershina, E., Sekelja, M., Linløkken, A., Wilson, R., and Rudi, K. (2014). Correlation between the human fecal microbiota and depression. *Neurogastroenterology & Motility*, 26(8), 1155-1162. doi:10.1111/nmo.12378

Rudd, M., Aaker, J., and Norton, M. I. (2014). Getting the most out of giving: Concretely framing a prosocial goal maximizes happiness. *Journal of Experimental Social Psychology*, 54, 11-24. doi:10.1016/j.jesp.2014.04.002

Nelson, S. K., Fuller, J. A., Choi, I., and Lyubomirsky, S. (2014). Beyond Self-Protection. *Personality and Social Psychology Bulletin*, 40(8), 998-1011. doi:10.1177/0146167214533389

Petrocchi, N., and Couyoumdjian, A. (2015). The impact of gratitude on depression and anxiety: The mediating role of criticizing, attacking, and reassuring the self. *Self and Identity*, 15(2), 191-205. doi:10.1080/15298868.2015.1095794

Frein, S. T., and Ponsler, K. (2013). Increasing Positive Affect in College Students. *Applied Research in Quality of Life*, 9(1), 1-13. doi:10.1007/s11482-013-9210-5

Rasciute, S., and Downward, P. (2010). Health or Happiness? What Is the Impact of Physical Activity on the Individual? *Kyklos*, 63(2), 256-270. doi:10.1111/j.1467-6435.2010.00472.x

Seligman, M. E. (2012). *Flourish*. North Sydney, NSW: Random House Australia.

Frankl, V. E., Boyne, J., and Winslade, W. J. (2006). *Man's Search for Meaning*. Boston: Beacon Press.

Corbyn, Z. (2017, January 29). Elizabeth Blackburn on the telomere effect: 'It's about keeping healthier for longer'. Retrieved from https://www.theguardian.com/science/2017/jan/29/telomere-effect-elizabeth-blackburn-nobel-prize-medicine-chromosomes

9 Steps. (n.d.). Retrieved from https://learningtoforgive.com/9-steps/

Wauters, A. (2010). *The Complete Guide to Chakras*. Hauppauge, NY: Barrons Educational Series.

Judith, A. (1999). *Wheels of Life: The Classic Guide to the Chakra System*. Woodbury, MN: Llewellyn Publications.

Csikszentmihalyi, M. (2009). *Flow: The Psychology of Optimal Experience*. New York: Harper Row.

Canadian Physical Activity Guidelines (n.d.) Retrieved from http://www.csep.ca/en/publications

Dishman, R. K., Berthoud, H., Booth, F. W., Cotman, C. W., Edgerton, V. R., Fleshner, M. R., . . . Zigmond, M. J. (2006). Neurobiology of Exercise*. *Obesity,14*(3), 345-356. doi:10.1038/oby.2006.46